Th
Ridgeway

National Trail Companion

supported by

5th edition published February 2008

© National Trails Office

ISBN 978-0-9535207-9-4

Edited by Jos Joslin & Diane Cooper

Photos on pages: 4 (top), 7, 8, 14, 19, 26, 27 (top),
33, 39 40, 53, 55, 56, 68, 74, 86, 89, 92
© *Tina Stallard/Natural England*
Photos on pages: 12, 20, 21, 22, 27 (bottom),
45, 48, 50, 59, 64, 69, 73, 81, 83, 93
© *Jos Joslin*
Photos on pages: 4 (bottom), 79, 80
© *Chilterns Conservation Board*

Published by

National Trails Office

Environment & Economy

Holton

Oxford OX33 1QQ

tel 01865 810224

fax 01865 810207

email Ridgeway@oxfordshire.gov.uk

website www.nationaltrail.co.uk

Designed by Linda Francis
tel 01865 407626

Printed by Cliffehanger Ltd
www.cliffehanger.co.uk

Cover photo:
Folly Clump, west of Letcombe Regis
© *Jos Joslin*

Contents

I   Introduction   5

II   History   8

III   Wildlife   9

IV   Who can use The Ridgeway   10

V   Preparing for your visit   11

VI   How to follow the Trail   13

     a. Guides   13

     b. Maps   13

     c. Signing   14

VII   Publications   15

VIII   Organised holidays   16

IX   Useful contacts   17

X   Getting there   20

XI   Follow the countryside code   21

XII   Emergency contacts   22

XIII   Accommodation, facilities & services   24

Section 1 – Overton Hill to Ogbourne St George   29

Section 2 – Ogbourne St George to Sparsholt Firs   41

Section 3 – Sparsholt Firs to Streatley   51

Section 4 – Streatley to Watlington   65

Section 5 – Watlington to Wendover   75

Section 6 – Wendover to Ivinghoe Beacon   87

Index of places   95

Distances between places   96

The Manger below Uffington Castle

The Chilterns Area of Outstanding Natural Beauty

Introduction

87 miles (139km) long, much of it following the ancient chalk ridge route used by prehistoric man and surrounded by numerous historic monuments, The Ridgeway offers the chance to get away from the bustle of life in this busy part of England. Perfect, but not too strenuous, for long distance use, this Trail is also ideal for day trips or less. The whole of The Ridgeway can be enjoyed by walkers with horseriders and cyclists able to use all of the western half as far as the River Thames at Streatley and short sections further east.

The Ridgeway

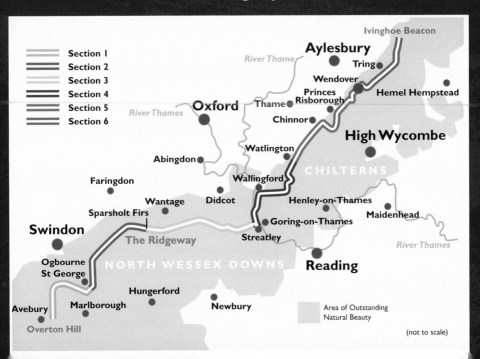

1 INTRODUCTION

This guide gives you all the information you need to plan an enjoyable visit to The Ridgeway. It has details about accommodation, refreshments, shops, transport, toilets and many other facilities along this National Trail.

The Companion is not a route guide: for detailed information about the Trail itself, The Ridgeway National Trail Guide by Anthony Burton (Aurum Press, 2007) is available from most book shops or online. Alternatively it can be mail ordered from the National Trails Office (see page 17 for details). The Companion complements the Trail Guide and, armed with a copy of each, it is hoped that anyone using The Ridgeway needn't require anything more. Enjoy your trip.

One of only 15 National Trails in England and Wales, The Ridgeway starts in the famous World Heritage Site of Avebury in Wiltshire. It travels for 87 miles (139km) steadily north east along the surprisingly remote scarp ridge of the downs, across the River Thames, and through the Chiltern Hills to finish in the Iron Age fort on top of Ivinghoe Beacon in Buckinghamshire.

The western half of The Ridgeway, as far as Streatley, can be enjoyed by walkers, horseriders and cyclists, whereas only walkers can use the full extent of the eastern half. Despite its relative remoteness, public transport to The Ridgeway is pretty good, especially to the eastern half, where there are several railway stations close to the Trail and an excellent bus network. With a little planning many places along the western half can also be reached by bus or train or a combination of the two.

The Ridgeway passes through two distinctive protected landscapes, both designated Areas of Outstanding Natural Beauty (AONB). The western half of the Trail travels through the open expansive downland of the North Wessex Downs AONB, whilst east of the Thames it stays amongst the more gentle and wooded countryside of the Chilterns AONB.

In the west The Ridgeway travels as a broad ancient track along the open and fairly isolated top of the chalk downland ridge, often several kilometres from the nearest village. Here, to the south is rolling downland and to the north, at the bottom of the steep scarp slope, the wide expanse of the Thames Valley. The far-reaching views are

dominated by the sky, the clouds and small clumps of beech woodland and all you may have for company is a solitary skylark singing overhead or a hare chasing across an adjacent field.

In the past these downs were sheep grazed, but since the introduction of fertilisers in the first half of the last century many areas have been ploughed and planted with crops. However sheep grazing does continue in places and, in others, a characteristic sight is immaculately managed grass tracks, the gallops used for training racehorses. The excellent turf of the downs makes this prime horse country but you need to be up early to see the strings of racehorses exercising.

At Streatley The Ridgeway crosses the River Thames and another of England's National Trails, the Thames Path, and enters more intimate and less open countryside. It follows the bank of the River Thames along a lovely 5 miles (8km) rural stretch before heading eastwards into the Chiltern Hills. Mostly on narrower paths, the Trail passes through woodlands, many of them beech, over neatly cultivated fields and across chalk grassland nature reserves rich in wildflowers. In contrast to the western half, although its usually peaceful here, you're never far from pleasant small towns or attractive villages.

With the support of Natural England, The Ridgeway is managed to the highest standards necessary for one of the most important paths in the country by the local highway authorities with a small dedicated team of staff and local volunteers.

Sheep on Pitstone Hill, Buckinghamshire

II HISTORY

For thousands of years, at least 5,000 and maybe many more, people have walked or ridden The Ridgeway, be they drovers, traders, invaders or today's recreational visitors. As part of a prehistoric track once stretching about 250 miles (400km) from the Dorset coast to the Wash on the Norfolk coast, The Ridgeway provided a route over the high ground for travellers which was less wooded and drier than routes through the springline villages below.

New Stone Age men, the first farmers in Britain, left the earliest remains. Their long barrows can be found at a few places both west and east of the River Thames. It was Bronze Age people from later times, around 2,000 BC, however, who dragged the huge sarsen stones from the surrounding hills and formed the dramatic Avebury Circle. There are many of their round burial barrows along the length of the National Trail.

Hill forts built during the Iron Age from about 500 BC until the Romans arrived in 43 AD are also found both sides of the Thames. These forts command the high ground and in several places they defended The Ridgeway against attack from the north.

In the Dark Ages The Ridgeway was a main route for the Saxons and Vikings who fought many battles during their advances into Wessex. In medieval times it was drovers driving livestock from Wales and the West Country to the Home Counties, not armies, who used The Ridgeway.

Until the Enclosure Acts of 1750 The Ridgeway was a broad band of tracks along the crest of the downs where travellers chose the driest or most convenient path. During Enclosures the exact course and width of The Ridgeway was defined by the building of earth banks and the planting of thorn hedges to prevent livestock straying into the newly cultivated fields.

In recent times use of The Ridgeway has changed greatly: farmers do still use much of it as an access route to their fields for tractors and other machinery but its main use is no longer utilitarian but recreational with walkers and riders out for exercise, pleasure and spiritual refreshment.

Avebury stones

The grasslands which occur on the chalk of the downs and the Chilterns are some of the most interesting habitats in England and some of the richest in terms of the number of plant species found. Chalk grassland has suffered from modern farming and much has disappeared under the plough. However those unimproved chalk grassland areas along The Ridgeway, especially the nature reserves east of the Thames, are well worth visiting where you'll find, amongst many other lovely plants, several types of orchid.

Another botanical treat in store for visitors during springtime is the carpet of bluebells in many of the woodlands in the Chilterns, usually in the first couple of weeks of May.

For those keen on seeing birds, The Ridgeway should not disappoint you. A range of relatively common birds such as warblers and finches are found the length of The Ridgeway enjoying the food supply provided by the hedges lining the Trail. Skylarks, yellowhammers and corn buntings are particularly characteristic of the downland and although generally in decline in Britain are still fairly numerous along The Ridgeway. The song of the corn bunting, likened to the sound of a jangle of keys, is the distinctive sound of the western half of The Ridgeway.

In colder months flocks of redwing and fieldfare, winter visitors from Scandinavia, are common and are usually seen feeding in the fields surrounding the Trail. However, most people will especially cherish the site of a red kite and you'll be unlucky if you don't see one in the Chiltern Hills and increasingly west of the Thames too. These magnificent birds of prey recognised by their forked tail were reintroduced to this area in the late 1980s and are now well established. In woodlands of this area too, woodpeckers and nuthatches may well be spotted.

Apart from the ubiquitous rabbit, hares and deer are the larger wild animals you may encounter. Hares are found in open countryside and are bigger than rabbits with longer ears and hind legs. They are solitary animals and most active at night, so late evening or early morning are the best times to see them. Two species of deer are found on The Ridgeway, roe and fallow with the former being the smaller and also living in smaller groups of just three or four animals. Both of these species are nocturnal and shy so, as for hares, being on The Ridgeway at dusk or dawn will give you the best chance of viewing them.

IV WHO CAN USE THE RIDGEWAY?

Walkers

Walkers can use the whole length of the Trail. There are also a series of circular walks available that use sections of The Ridgeway (see page 15 for details)

Cyclists and Horseriders

Riders, both cyclists and horseriders, can share The Ridgeway with walkers all the way from the start at Overton Hill near Avebury to Streatley on the River Thames, a distance of roughly 43 miles (68km). Once across the river the only long section of the Trail which can be ridden is the 8-miles (13-km) stretch which follows the Icknield Way through the Chilterns from Britwell Hill near Watlington to Wainhill on the Oxfordshire/Buckinghamshire border. In other places The Ridgeway is a footpath and it is a trespass offence to ride on a footpath without the permission of the landowner.

However an alternative for riders is to join the Swan's Way long distance bridleway at Goring-on-Thames, just across the river from Streatley, and to follow this mostly on The Ridgeway to Bledlow west of Princes Risborough (here the Swan's Way turns north). From Bledlow riders can pick up the Icknield Way Riders' Route which provides a good alternative to The Ridgeway for riders as far as Pitstone Hill, just a couple of kilometres from Ivinghoe Beacon. Unfortunately riders can't continue to Ivinghoe Beacon, the official end of the National Trail, since the route to it is on footpaths.

There are some circular rides for cyclists and horseriders that use sections of The Ridgeway (see page 15 for details)

Vehicles

Until May 2006 recreational vehicles were legally allowed to use considerable amounts of The Ridgeway, but now they can only use about 20% (17 miles) of it and, apart from two short sections, only from May until the end of September each year. So if you visit The Ridgeway during the summer, as well as encountering some agricultural vehicles be prepared to see the odd motorbike or four-wheel drive, particularly at the western end of the Trail.

Deciding where to start

The Ridgeway can be walked in either direction and is signposted both ways. The route is generally promoted from west to east, starting at Overton Hill and finishing on Ivinghoe Beacon, because prevailing winds tend to come from the southwest and so will be behind you.

How far to walk in a day

How far you walk in a day is obviously up to you and will depend on your fitness and experience. As a guide, people generally walk at about 2½ miles (4km) an hour but on sections with climbs and descents slightly longer should be allowed. If you are planning to walk the whole length of The Ridgeway, or for several days, it is usually sensible to plan a short first day to ease yourself in gently.

What to take with you

- Carry warm and waterproof clothing as even on some summer days wind and rain can make a walk or ride uncomfortable.

- Walkers should wear strong, comfortable footwear. During the summer trainers are usually OK for a walk on The Ridgeway, but during wet periods and winter months don walking boots or even Wellingtons if you're comfortable walking in these. Take a blister repair kit, just in case.

- Wear protection (hat and lotion) against the sun during the summer – the western half of the Trail is particularly exposed.

- Carry water if walking or riding for more than a couple of hours – water points west of the River Thames are relatively infrequent.

- If your walk or ride is along unfamiliar paths don't forget your map and/or guidebook!

V PREPARING FOR YOUR VISIT

Personal safety

If you are walking/riding alone it's sensible, as a simple precaution, to let someone know where you are and when you expect to arrive/return. Do bear in mind that mobile phone coverage can be patchy in rural areas, so you cannot always rely on them.

 ### Dog Matters

If you are planning to undertake a long distance walk along The Ridgeway with your dog, you are advised to ensure it is fit before you start; on occasions walkers have had to abandon a walk because their dogs can't keep up!

Please also make sure your dog is under close control at all times to prevent it from disturbing livestock or wildlife. You are asked to keep your dog on a lead when you're in the few fields you'll encounter with livestock, although if you find that cattle seriously harass you because of the dog, it may be wise to let it off the lead.

12

The Official National Trail Guide

The Ridgeway National Trail Guide by Anthony Burton, Aurum Press 2007. The official guide to the Trail with written route description and colour 1:25,000 Ordnance Survey maps. Costs £12.99 and is available from the National Trails Office (see page 17)

Other Guides

Details of other guides and publications are on page 15

Maps

It is usually a good idea to use maps when walking, particularly in unfamiliar areas. The official National Trail Guide includes colour sections of all the appropriate 1:25 000 Ordnance Survey maps needed to follow The Ridgeway. Alternatively, for you to enjoy and interpret the wider landscape, you may wish to purchase your own Ordnance Survey maps.

The Landranger series (pink cover at 1:50 000 or 2cm to 1km) has all public rights of way, viewpoints, tourist information and selected places of interest marked on them. For the whole of The Ridgeway you will need:

173   Swindon and Devizes
174   Newbury and Wantage
175   Reading and Windsor
165   Aylesbury and Leighton Buzzard

The larger scale Explorer series (orange cover at 1:25 000 or 4cm to 1km) has more detail including fence lines which can be very helpful when following rights of way, recreational routes and greater tourist information. For the whole of The Ridgeway you will need:

157   Marlborough and Savernake Forest
170   Abingdon, Wantage and Vale of White Horse
171   Chiltern Hills West
181   Chiltern Hills North

Signage

The Ridgeway follows a series of well signed public rights of way and minor roads (91% of the Trail is off road).

The acorn is the symbol of National Trails and is used on all Ridgeway signage. In most cases the signs, or waymark discs on gates or posts, will also carry the word 'Ridgeway'. The status of the right of way, which defines who can use it, will also be shown either in words, or by using the national waymarking scheme of coloured arrows – see below:

 Footpath

 Bridleway

 Restricted Byway

 Byway

The downs near Wantage

Publications About The Ridgeway

National Trails Office contact details are on page 16

The Ridgeway National Trail Guide by Anthony Burton, Aurum Press 2007 - the official guide with written route description from Overton Hill to Ivinghoe Beacon and colour 1:25 000 maps. Available from the National Trails Office.

Ridgeway, Harvey Maps, 2003 - 1:40 000 scale waterproof map of the entire route of The Ridgeway including information on a range of facilities along the Trail. Available from the National Trails Office.

Exploring the Ridgeway by Alan Charles, Countryside Books 2000 - based on 14 circular walks covering the whole length of The Ridgeway from Ivinghoe Beacon to Overton Hill.

The Oldest Road - an Exploration of the Ridgeway by J R L Anderson with photographs by Fay Godwin. Paperback edition by Whittet Books, 1992.

Walking in Britain, Lonely Planet, 2007 - includes a description of the western half of The Ridgeway.

The Greater Ridgeway by Ray Quinlan, Cicerone, 2003. Describes a route from Lyme Regis to Hunstanton, including The Ridgeway National Trail.

Ridgeway Information (Heritage) Pack - leaflets about the history and wildlife of The Ridgeway. Available from the National Trails Office.

Walks around The Ridgeway Pack - leaflets describing circular and other walks from The Ridgeway. Available from the National Trails Office.

Riding Routes around The Ridgeway Pack - leaflets describing circular rides from The Ridgeway. Available from the National Trails Office.

Let's Hear it for The Ridgeway! by Elizabeth Newbery - a family activity book full of ideas and information on things to do and see on and close to The Ridgeway. Available from the National Trails Office.

Events Programme - a range of guided events around The Ridgeway. Free from the National Trails Office.

VIII ORGANISED HOLIDAYS

The following companies offer self-guided or guided holiday packages on part or all of The Ridgeway.

Walking

Contours Walking Holidays, Gramyre, 3 Berrier Road, Greystoke, CA11 0UB. **T**: 01768 480451 www.contours.co.uk - 7-night self-guided package from £415.

Explore Britain, 6 George St, Ferryhill DL17 0DT. **T**: 01740 650900 www.xplorebritain.com - 5, 6, or 9 nights self-guided packages start from £343.

Freedom Walking Holidays, 4 Almond Court, Swanpool, Lincoln LN6 0HD. **T**: 01522 684104 www.freedom-walking.co.uk

Cycling

Rough Tracks, Alexandra Road, Frome BA11 1LX. **T**: 07000 560749 www.rough-tracks.co.uk - weekend guided tour in Wiltshire including part of The Ridgeway.

Horse Riding

Pewsey Vale Riding Centre, Church Farm, Stanton St Bernard, Marlborough SN8 4LJ **T**: 01672 851400 - www.pewseyvaleridingcentre.com - 1 or 2-day ride from Pewsey to Streatley.

Bridle Rides Ltd, PO Box 9223, Bromsgrove B60 1PF. **T**: 0121 445 6998 www.bridlerides.co.uk - 2-5 day rides along the western half of The Ridgeway for those riding their own horse.

Please note for those visiting The Ridgeway independently many of the accommodation providers listed in this guide are willing to collect you from and return you to The Ridgeway. Many will also transport your luggage to your next night's accommodation.

The Ridgeway Managers and National Trails Office

Margaret Caddick and Jos Joslin, National Trails Office, Environment & Economy, Holton, Oxford OX33 1QQ. **T**: 01865 810224. **F**: 01865 810207.
E: Nationaltrails@oxfordshire.gov.uk

Highway Authorities responsible for public rights of way

Buckinghamshire County Council, Rights of Way, County Hall, Walton Street, Aylesbury HP20 1UY. **T**: 0845 370 8090 www.buckscc.gov.uk

Hertfordshire County Council, Planning and Environment, County Hall, Hertford SG13 8DQ. **T**: 01923 471555 www.hertsdirect.org

Oxfordshire County Council, Countryside Service, Environment and Economy, Holton, Oxford OX33 1QQ. **T**: 01865 810226 www.oxfordshire.gov.uk

Swindon Borough Council, Highways Department, Premier House, Station Road, Swindon SN1 1TZ. **T**: 01793 463000 www.swindon.gov.uk

West Berkshire Council, Countryside and Environment, Faraday Road, Newbury RG14 5LD. **T**: 01635 42400 www.westberks.gov.uk

Wiltshire County Council, Dept of Environmental Services, County Hall, Trowbridge, Wilts BA14 8JN. **T**: 01225 713000 www.wiltshire.gov.uk

Agency responsible for National Trails

Natural England, South East Region, 11 Fenlock Court, Blenheim Office Park, Long Hanborough OX29 8LN **T**: 01993 886540 www.naturalengland.org.uk

Areas of Outstanding Natural Beauty

North Wessex Downs AONB Office, Denford Manor, Hungerford RG17 0UN.
T: 01488 685440 www.northwessexdowns.org.uk

Chilterns Conservation Board, The Lodge, Station Road, Chinnor OX39 4HA
T: 01844 355500 www.chilternsaonb.org

IX USEFUL CONTACTS

Organisations for walkers

Backpackers Club, **E**: inforequest@backpackersclub.co.uk
www.backpackersclub.co.uk

Long Distance Walkers Association, Membership Secretary, 7 Shetland Way, Radcliffe, Manchester M26 4UH **E**: membership@lwda.org.uk www.ldwa.org.uk

Oxford Fieldpaths Society, c/o Membership Secretary, 28 Harpes Road, Oxford OX2 7QL. **T**: 01865 553699 www.ofs.org.uk

Ramblers Association, 2nd Floor, Camelford House, 87-90 Albert Embankment, London SE1 7TW **T**: 020 7339 8500 www.ramblers.org.uk

Organisations for cyclists

British Cycling Federation, National Cycling Centre, Stuart Street, Manchester M11 4DQ.**T**: 0870 8712000 **E**: info@britishcycling.org.uk www.britishcycling.org.uk

Cyclists Touring Club (Off-Road), CTC, Parklands, Railton Road, Guildford GU2 9JX.**T**: 0870 873 0060 **E**: cycling@ctc.org.uk www.ctc.org.uk

Sustrans, 2 Cathedral Square, College Green, Bristol BS1 5DD. **T**: 0117 926 8893 **E**: info@sustrans.org.uk www.sustrans.org.uk

The Rough Stuff Fellowship, New Members Secretary, 8 Beech Road, Holton LA2 6QQ **T**: 01524 811843 **E**: dsorme@REMOVEtiscali.co.uk

Organisations for horseriders

British Horse Society, Stoneleigh Deer Park, Kenilworth CV8 2XZ.
T: 0870 120 2244 **E**: enquiry@bhs.org.uk www.bhs.org.uk

Byways & Bridleways Trust, PO Box 117, Newcastle upon Tyne NE3 5YT. www. bbtrust.org.uk

Endurance GB, National Agricultural Centre, Stoneleigh Park, Kenilworth CV8 2RP. **T**: 02476 698863 **E**: enquiries@endurancegb.co.uk www.endurancegb.co.uk

Tourist Information providers

Details of these are included in the introductory pages to each of the six sections of The Ridgeway.

Other organisations

Berkshire, Buckinghamshire & Oxfordshire Wildlife Trust, The Lodge, I Armstrong Road, Littlemore, Oxford OX4 4XT. **T**: 01865 775476 **E**: info@bbowt.org.uk www.bbowt.org.uk

Chiltern Society, White Hill Centre, White Hill Chesham, HP5 IAG. **T**: 01494 771250 **E**: office@chilternsociety.org.uk www.chilternsociety.org.uk

Friends of the Ridgeway, c/o Jeff Goddard, 6 Darell Road, Caversham, Reading RG4 7AY. **E**: jandjgoddard@googlemail.com www.ridgewayfriends.org.uk

Herts & Middlesex Wildlife Trust, Grebe House, St Michael's Street, St Albans AL3 4SN. **T**: 01727 858901 **E**: info@hmwt.org www.wildlifetrust.org.uk/herts

Wiltshire Wildlife Trust, Elm Tree Court, Long Street, Devizes, SN10 INJ. **T**: 01380 725670 **E**: info@wiltshirewildlife.org www.wiltshirewildlife.org

Waylands Smithy long barrow

19

X GETTING THERE

Getting to The Ridgeway by public transport is fairly easy, particularly the eastern half of the Trail, and a useful map-based leaflet showing relevant public transport routes is available free from the National Trails Office (see page 17 for details).

Alternatively, telephone numbers and websites to find out more about public transport to the Trail are listed below:

* Rail Services 08457 484950 (24 hours a day)
  www.nationalrail.co.uk

* Bus Services 0871 2002233
  www.traveline.org.uk

* Taxi Services Information is included in each of the six sections

We encourage people to consider using public transport rather than travelling by private car as this is better for the environment, helps to support local public transport services and reduces congestion from parking in the smaller settlements. However, those wishing to travel to The Ridgeway by car are asked to park considerately if parking in villages on or close to the Trail. Other places to park are listed within each section.

• Be safe – plan ahead and follow any signs

Even when going out locally, it's best to get the latest information about where and when you can go. Follow advice and local signs, and be prepared for the unexpected.

• Leave gates and property as you find them

Please respect the working life of the countryside, as our actions can affect people's livelihoods, our heritage, and the safety and welfare of animals and ourselves.

• Protect plants and animals, and take your litter home

We have a responsibility to protect our countryside now and for future generations, so make sure you don't harm animals, birds, plants or trees.

• Keep your dog under close control

The countryside is a great place to exercise dogs, but it's every owner's duty to make sure their dog is not a danger or nuisance to farm animals, wildlife or other people.

• Consider other people

Showing consideration and respect for other people makes the countryside a pleasant environment for everyone – at home, at work and at leisure.

For further details visit www.countrysideaccess.gov.uk

From Lodge Hill, southwest of Princes Risborough

XII EMERGENCY CONTACTS

We hope you will not need to refer to this page during your visit but the information below will help you find the service you need quickly should something unforeseen occur. In urgent and life threatening situations, or when a crime is in progress, the emergency services can be contacted on **999 or 112**.

When the situation is not an emergency please use the following contact details:

Police

To contact local police stations, telephone the number relevant to the section/ county you are in and ask to be put through to the nearest police station.

Section	County	Tel Number
1&2	Wiltshire	01380 735735
2-6	Oxfordshire, Berkshire & Buckinghamshire	08458 505505
6	Hertfordshire	08458 33002225

Grim's Ditch east of Wallingford during Spring

Hospitals

The following hospitals with casualty departments are located in the places shown below. The telephone numbers given are the hospital switchboard; ask to be put through to Accident and Emergency Reception.

◆ Full 24-hour emergency service

▲ Minor injuries only, NOT 24-hour service

Section	Town	Telephone No	Address
1	▲ Devizes	01380 723511	Devizes Hospital, New Park Road, Devizes (daily 8am-10pm)
1&2	▲ Marlborough	01672 517200	Savernake Hospital, London Road, Marlborough (daily 8am-10pm)
1&2	◆ Swindon	01793 604020	The Great Western Hospital, Marlborough Road, Swindon
3&4	◆ Oxford	01865 741166	John Radcliffe Hospital Headley Way, Headington Oxford OX3 9DU
3&4	▲ Wallingford	01491 208500	Wallingford Community Hospital, Reading Road, Wallingford (daily 9am-5pm)
5&6	◆ Aylesbury	01296 315000	Stoke Mandeville Hospital, Mandeville Road, Aylesbury

XIII ACCOMMODATION, FACILITIES & SERVICES

The following chapters give details of the settlements, accommodation, eating places, shops, attractions and other facilities along or near The Ridgeway. They are listed in geographic order from Overton Hill to Ivinghoe Beacon.

The Ridgeway is divided into six sections as indicated on the map on page 5. At the start of each section is a map showing the settlements close to the Trail within that section. These maps are meant only as a guide and you are recommended to use this Companion in conjunction with The Ridgeway National Trail Guide or maps.

If you fail to find accommodation using this guide please contact the Tourist Information providers listed near the beginning of each section which may be able to provide other addresses.

You are strongly advised to book accommodation in advance. Whilst booking, do check prices since those quoted here are usually the minimum charged.

For those who would like to enjoy more than a day on The Ridgeway without having to carry all their possessions, many accommodation providers have indicated whether they are willing to transport the luggage you don't need during the day to your next night's accommodation. The fee charged for this service needs to be discussed and agreed at the time of the booking. Accommodation providers have also indicated if they are willing to collect you from The Ridgeway and deliver you back after your stay.

All the information within this Companion is as accurate as possible. Inclusion of accommodation does not constitute a recommendation although it is indicated in the details whether an establishment has a recognised grade awarded to it. If you have any comments or notice any errors, please write to Jos Joslin the National Trails Manager (page 17).

Camping on The Ridgeway

The situation regarding camping on The Ridgeway is, in theory, clear enough; The Ridgeway is privately owned and the public right of way along it is for passage only, not for stopping and camping.

In practice, however, most landowners do not object if a tent is pitched on The Ridgeway for a night and disappears the next morning as long as no litter is left, no damage done, nor camp fires lit. Do not camp in adjoining fields, woods or gallops without prior permission from the landowner.

Key to Symbols for Settlements

Any comments relate to preceding icon.

	map grid reference (see start of each section for relevant maps)
	shortest walking distance from The Ridgeway
	most convenient train station
P£	car park (paying)
PF	car park (free)
	telephone
	toilets
&WC	toilets adapted for disabled users
	Tourist Information Centre
	pub (usually open lunchtimes 11am-3pm then evenings 6pm-11pm). Names and telephone numbers of pubs are given for those settlements with up to two pubs
✕	bar meals in pub
✉	post office (usual opening hours 9am-5.30pm weekdays; 9:00-12.30pm Sat)
	general store (usual opening hours daily 9am-5.30pm Mon-Sat)
	cafe/tea shop
	restaurant
	food take-away

opening hours of services relate to the preceding symbol

S M T W T F S

eg: open all day

closed all day

Post offices, general stores, cafe/tea shops - open morning; Pubs, bar meals, restaurants, takeaways - open lunchtime

Post offices, general stores, cafe/tea shops - open afternoon; Pubs, bar meals, restaurants, takeaways - open evening

£	bank (usually open daily 9.30am-4.30pm Mon-Fri)
	cash machine available, including outside bank opening hours
☆	tourist attraction

Key to Symbols for Accommodation

Type of accommodation (symbols in margins)

▲	hostel	B&B	bed and breakfast
⚑	camping	U	horse accommodation
Ⓗ	hotel	SC	self catering
INN	inn		

Tom Brown's School Museum, Uffington

The number and price following the symbols for rooms gives the number and price of that type of room available. The same applies to tent/caravan pitches and stabling/grazing for horses. Prices quoted for rooms are the minimum price per room per night for bed and breakfast. The price for single occupancy of double, twin or family rooms is given in brackets eg (£30.00).

Accommodation symbols - hotels, inns, guest houses, B&Bs and youth hostels

🛏	double room	◐	evening meals available by arrangement
🛏	twin room	(G)	grazing for horses
🛏	family room	(S)	stabling for horses
🛏	single room	🚲	secure cycle storage
⊖	smoking bedroom(s) available	**DRY**	clothes/boots drying facilities
👫	children welcome	⬚	laundry facilities
♿	wheelchair access	🚗	transport to and from Trail by arrangement
🐕	dogs allowed by arrangement		
V	caters for vegetarians	🚶	luggage transported to next overnight stop by arrangement
●	most food locally sourced		
◗	some food locally sourced	💳	credit card(s) accepted
●	most food is organic	★	VisitBritain accommodation standard
○	some food is organic		
🍴	packed lunches available	🚩	special feature/comment

Accommodation symbols - camping and caravan sites

⛺	tent pitches	🚿	showers
🚐	caravan pitches	📞	public telephone
🚰	cold water	⬚	laundry facilities
🚰	hot water	🏪	site shop
🚻	toilets	CG	camping gas
♿WC	toilets adapted for disabled users	🚩	special feature/comment

27

Hackpen Hill, Wiltshire

Smeathe's Ridge

Section 1

Overton Hill to Ogbourne St George

Starting in the Avebury World Heritage Site with its wealth
of archaeology, this 9.3 miles (14.8km) stretch of The Ridgeway
climbs gradually to a high point at Barbury Castle Iron Age fort.
From there the route along Smeathe's Ridge provides great views
on either side as it gently descends to the valley of the River Og.

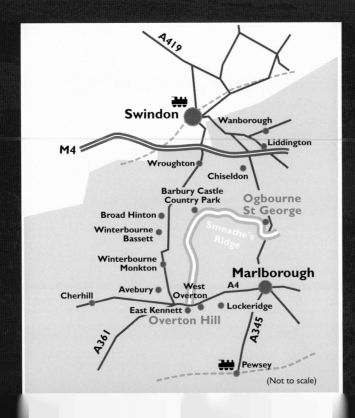

(Not to scale)

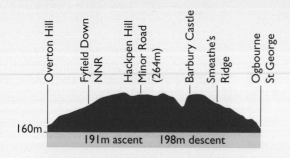

Overton Hill | Fyfield Down NNR | Hackpen Hill Minor Road (264m) | Barbury Castle | Smeathe's Ridge | Ogbourne St George

160m

191m ascent   198m descent

Maps

| Landranger maps | 173 | Swindon and Devizes |
| Explorer maps | 157 | Marlborough and Savernake Forest |

Taxis

Place	Name	Telephone Number
Marlborough	Arrow Private Hire	01672 515567
	Kayze Cars	01672 514556
	Marlborough Radio Cars	01672 511088
	Marlborough Taxis	01672 512786
	Merlin Car Service	01672 861000
	Paddy's Taxis	01672 511884
	Travel Far	01672 513274

Car Parking

If you choose to park in villages close to The Ridgeway, please park considerately. Other places to park are listed below but you need to be aware that theft from cars parked in the countryside does occur. You are advised to leave any unnecessary items at home or, failing that, ensure that anything valuable is locked in the boot of your vehicle.

Place	Map Grid Reference
On Ridgeway at the start at Overton Hill, on north side of A4, 4¹/₂ miles (7km) west of Marlborough	SU 119681
On Ridgeway at Hackpen Hill on minor road between Marlborough and Broad Hinton, 2 miles (3km) east of Broad Hinton	SU 129747
On Ridgeway at Barbury Castle Country Park, 5 miles (8km) south of Swindon signed from Wroughton and Chiseldon	SU 157762

Water Points

Place	Map Grid Reference
Barbury Castle Country Park (at the café)	SU 158760

Toilets

Place	Map Grid Reference
Barbury Castle Country Park	SU 155762

Vets

* large animal vets

Place	Name	Telephone Number
Marlborough	The Drove Veterinary Hospital	01672 512043
	Riverside Veterinary Centre*	01672 514875

Farriers

Place	Name	Telephone Number
Marlborough	J Baker	01672 514013
	I Buck	07702 512288
	AP Marshall	07053 518057
	ND Quinlan	07847 344670
	AJ Turnell	07768 535271
Aldbourne	Peter Baker	01672 540812
Wroughton	P A Groom	01793 814185

Saddlers

Place	Name	Telephone Number
Marlborough	G & S Saddlery	01672 515665
Swindon	The Tack Shop	01672 811366

Riding Stables for Guided Rides

Place	Name	Telephone Number
Marlborough	Pewsey Vale Riding Centre	01672 851400
Chiseldon	Lady Smith Equestrian Centre	01793 740842

Horsebox Parking

The following places have sufficient space for you to park your horsebox. You **must** call in advance to arrange as space may be scarce. A fee may also be charged.

Place	Name	Telephone Number
Marlborough	Brown's Farm (Accommodation guests and day-riders)	01672 515129
Wroughton	Hackpen Liveries (Accommodation guests and day-riders)	01793 845024
Ogbourne St George	Foxlynch (Accommodation guests)	01672 841307
	Lower Herdswick Farm (Accommodation guests)	01672 841166
	Parklands Hotel (Accommodation guests and day-riders)	01672 841555

Bike Repairs

Place	Name	Telephone Number
Marlborough	Acceler8 Cycles	01672 513414
	Bertie Muffoons	01672 519119
Swindon	Bike Doctor	01793 874873
	Dans Bike Bits	01793 423380
	Mitchell Cycles	01793 523306
	Park South People Centre	01793 485518
	Red Planet Bikes	01793 519119
	Swindon Cycles Superstore	01793 700105
	Total Bike	01793 644185

Mountain Bike Hire

Place	Name	Telephone Number
Marlborough	Acceler8 Cycles	01672 513414
Swindon	Swindon Cycles Superstore (local delivery and car rack hire)	01793 700105

Tourist Information Centres

These TICs are staffed but note that many libraries in the area have leaflets about local attractions and events.
★ offers accommodation booking service

Place	Address/Opening Hours
Avebury	Avebury Chapel Centre, Green Street, Avebury SN8 1RE T: 01672 539425 F: 01672 539296 E: all.tic's@kennet.gov.uk W: www.visitkennet.co.uk Opening hours: Summer (Easter-31 Oct) Tues-Sun 9:30-17:00 Winter (1 Nov-Easter) Wed-Sun 9:30-16:30
★Swindon	37 Regent Street, Swindon SN1 1JL T: 01793 530328 F: 01793 434031 E: infocentre@swindon.gov.uk W: www.visitswindon.co.uk Opening hours: All year: Mon-Sat 09:15-17:00

Autumn ploughing

Browns Farm

Marlborough, Wilts
Tel 01672 515129

Peaceful farmhouse set on the edge of Savernake Forest.
B&B accommodation: Tea/coffee facilities, some with en-suite facilities.
TV Lounge and large gardens available for guests.

 Also 2 self contained
properties for
self catering.

Ideal base for touring Wiltshire. Immediate access to footpaths &
bridleways. Working Beef/Arable Farm. Ample off-street parking

MARLBOROUGH

☼ SU1969 🥾 4.4 miles (7km)
🚂 Swindon 11 miles (18km) 🚻

Town with full range of services. Visit www.visitkennet.co.uk for further details, including information about a range of accommodation.

RB ∪
5C

Browns Farm

✢ GR SU198678 0.9miles(1.5km) south of Marlborough
Mrs Hazel J Crockford
Browns Farm, Marlborough SN8 4ND
T: 01672 515129 **M:** 07931 311985
E: crockford@farming.co.uk
www. marlboroughholidaycottages.co.

🛏️ I £45 🛏️ I £37 🛏️ I £44 (£25)

Most major cards. Some rooms en-suite
Ⓢ 2 £10 Ⓖ 4 £10
🏇 2 self contained properties for self-catering also available from £200/week ★★★ Horsebox parking available for day-riders

LOCKERIDGE

☼ SU1467 🥾 1.6 miles (2.5km)
🚂 Swindon 14.6 miles (23.5km)
📞

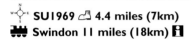
S M T W T F S   S M T W T F S

Pub: Who'd A Thought It Inn 01672 861255

Taffrail   *closed Dec*   B&B

Mrs Julie Spencer
Back Lane, Lockeridge, Marlborough
SN8 4ED
T/F: 01672 861266
E: spencer@taffrail.eclipse.co.uk

🛏️ I £40 🛏️ 2 £40 (£25)
🏇 (over 7) V 🍴 🚲 DRY 🅿️ 🚗 🥾

WEST OVERTON

☼ SU1367 🥾 0.6 miles (1km)
🚂 Swindon 13 miles (21km) 📞

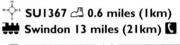

S M T W T F S   S M T W T F S

Pub: Bell Inn 01672 861663

EAST KENNETT

☼ SU1267 🥾 0.4 miles (0.7km)
🚂 Pewsey 11 miles (18km) 📞

Old Forge   *closed Xmas & New Year*   B&B

Mrs L Feeley
East Kennett, Marlborough SN8 4EY
T: 01672 861686 **M:** 07770 871066
F: 01672 861136 **E:** laura@feeleyfamily.
fsnet.co.uk
www.theoldforge.mysite.wanadoo-members.co.uk

🛏️ I £45 🛏️ I £60 🚫 🏇 🄶 V 🦽
🚲 DRY 🅿️ 🚗 🥾 ★★★★
Some rooms en-suite
🏆 VisitBritain Silver Award

35

AVEBURY

SU1069 ⌂ **1.2 miles (2km)**
Swindon 12 miles (20km) PF
📞 ⑯ 🅷

🍺 ||||||||||| ✕ |||||||||||
  S M T W T F S   S M T W T F S

✉ |||||||||| 🧺 |||||||||||
  S M T W T F S   S M T W T F S

🫖 |||||||||||
  S M T W T F S

Pub: Red Lion 01672 539266

☆ Avebury World Heritage Site
T: 01672 539250 www.nationaltrust.
org.uk

☆ Alexander Keiller Museum
T: 01672 539250
www.nationaltrust.org.uk

B&B Manor Farm *closed Xmas & Easter*

Mrs Judith Farthing
Avebury, Marlborough SN8 1RF
T/F: 01672 539294

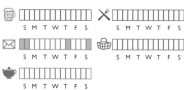 1 £80 🛏 1 £80 (£60) 👫 (over
11) V 🎒 🚲 ★★★★

🅷 Private bathroom

Avebury Lodge   B&B

Mr Andrew Blackall
The Lodge, High Street, Avebury,
Marlborough SN8 1RF
T: 01672 539023 **F:** 01672 539142
E: avebury@email.com
www.aveburylodge.co.uk
🛏 2 £225 🛏 1 £225 🛏 1 £250
(£95) 👫 V 🐾 🎒 🟦 Mastercard, Visa.
Some rooms en-suite

WINTERBOURNE MONKTON

SU1072 ⌂ **1.9 miles (3km)**
Swindon 9 miles (15km) PF 📞

New Inn B&B *closed Xmas & New Year* B&B

Sandra Pope
The New Inn, Winterbourne Monkton,
Swindon SN4 9NW
T: 01672 539240 **M:** 07890 948726
E: enquiries@thenewinn.net
www.thenewinn.net

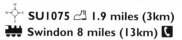 2 £60 🛏 2 £60 🛏 1 £65 (£50)

 👫 ⚷ V 🎒 📞 O 🚲 DRY 🖥 🚗
🎒 🟦 Most major cards. ★★★ All
rooms en-suite

WINTERBOURNE BASSETT

SU1075 ⌂ **1.9 miles (3km)**
Swindon 8 miles (13km) 📞

🍺 ||||||||||| ✕ |||||||||||
  S M T W T F S   S M T W T F S

Pub: White Horse Inn 01793 731257

BROAD HINTON

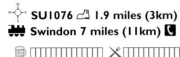 **SU1076** 1.9 miles (3km)
Swindon 7 miles (11km) 📞

| | |
| S M T W T F S | S M T W T F S |

| | |
| S M T W T F S | S M T W T F S |

in Post Office
Pubs: Crown Inn 01793 731302 & Bell
Inn 01793 731251

BARBURY CASTLE

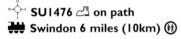 **SU1476** on path
Swindon 6 miles (10km) 👬

| |
| S M T W T F S |

☆ Barbury Castle Country Park
T: 01793 490150 www.swindon.gov.
uk/barbury

⚠ Barbury Castle Camping *closed weekdays in winter*

Mrs Antonioy
Ridgeway Farm, Wroughton, Swindon
SN4 0QH
T: 01793 845346
⚠ 20 £10 (including breakfast)
👬 🔌
🍴 Packed lunche provided and a
covered outdoor eating area

WROUGHTON

 **SU1480** 2.5 miles (4km)
Swindon 3 miles (5km)PF 📞
👬 ♿WC

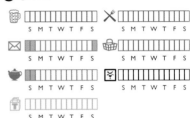

| | |
| S M T W T F S | S M T W T F S |

| | |
| S M T W T F S | S M T W T F S |

| | |
| S M T W T F S | S M T W T F S |

| |
| S M T W T F S |

Outside Co-Op
☆ Science Museum Wroughton
T: 01793 846200 www.voteinspired.
org.uk

Artis Cottage Guesthouse B&B

Miss Kirsty Heather
1 Swindon Road, Wroughton, Swindon
SN4 9AG
T: 01793 845424 **M:** 07974 665529
E: kirstyheather@aol.com
www.artis-cottage-guesthouse.co.uk
🛏 3 £55 🛏 1 £55 🛏 1 £70 (£35)
🛏 1 £35 👫 V ♿ 🌑 🚲 🚗 All
rooms en-suite

Hackpen Liveries ♘

Mr & Mrs Glen & Fiona Symes
2 Hackpen Farm Cottages, Wroughton,
Swindon SN4 0QZ
T: 01793 845024 **M:** 07778 103032
🅢 8 £7 🅖 20 £5
🍴 Call in advance to arrange horsebox
parking for guests and day-riders

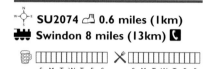

CHISELDON

SU1879 ⌂ 1.9 miles (3km)
🍺 Swindon 5 miles (8km) **PF** ☎

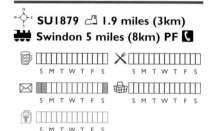

☆ Chiseldon Museum **T**: 01793 740432

Ⓗ **Chiseldon House Hotel** *closed Xmas*

Mrs Sue Higgs
New Road, Chiseldon, Swindon
SN4 0NE
T: 01793 741010 **F**: 01793 741059
E: info@chiseldonhousehotel.co.uk
www.chiseldonhousehotel.co.uk
🛏 15 £110 🛏 5 £110 (£90) 🛏 1 £90
⚥ ♿ ▧ V ⚘ ❍ ● ○ ☎ **DRY** ▣
🐾 💳 Most major cards ★★★ All
rooms en-suite

B&B **Courtleigh House**   *closed Xmas & New Year*

Mrs Ruth Hibberd
40 Draycot Road, Chiseldon, Swindon
SN4 0LS
T: 01793 740246
E: courtleighhouse@yahoo.co.uk
🛏 2 £60 (£30) 🛏 1 £30 ⚥ V ⚘
☎ **DRY** ▣ ⚘ 🐾 ★★★★ Some
rooms en-suite
◀ VisitBritain Silver Award

OGBOURNE ST GEORGE

SU2074 ⌂ 0.6 miles (1km)
🍺 Swindon 8 miles (13km) ☎

Pubs: Inn With The Well 01672 841445
& Parklands Hotel 01672 841555

Blue Barn B&B   B&B

Mrs Jackie Palmer
Ogbourne St George, Marlborough SN8
2NT
T: 01672 841082 **M**: 07770 975965
E: jax@capalmer.co.uk
www.blue.barn.co.uk
🛏 1 £65 🛏 1 £65* (£45) ⚥ ▧ V
⚘ ❍ ☎ **DRY** ▣ ⚘ 🐾 ★★★★
◀ *£20 extra/person more than
2 in family room. Self-catering
accommodation also available @ £65
per unit

Parklands Hotel & Bentleys Restaurant   Ⓗ

Mr Mark Bentley
High Street, Ogbourne St George,
Marlborough SN8 1SL
T: 01672 841555 **F**: 01672 841533
E: mark@parklandshoteluk.co.uk
www.parklandshoteluk.co.uk
🛏 6 £75 🛏 4 £75 🛏 1 £90 (£40)
🛏 1 £55 ⚥ (over 9) ♿ V ⚘ ☎ ⚘
DRY 🐾 💳 Most major cards ★★★★
All rooms en-suite
Ⓢ 2 £10
◀ Call in advance to arrange horsebox
parking for guests and day-riders

B&B | **Sanctuary**

Mrs Rebecca MacDonald
Ogbourne St George, Marlborough SN8
1SQ
T: 01672 841473 **M:** 07850 325344
E: rebecca.macdonald@core-support.
co.uk   www.the-sanctuary.biz
🛏 1 £60 🛏 1 £60 🛏 1 £75 (£45)
⚥ 🗎 V ♿ 🖑 🚲 DRY 🔄 👣 ★★★★
Some rooms en-suite
🍴 Evening meals not available on winter
Sundays

Foxlynch   **B&B** ♈

Mr G Edwins
Ogbourne St George, Marlborough
SN8 1TD
T: 01672 841307
🛏 1 £40 🛏 1 £20/person 🛏 1 £20
⚥ 🗎 V ♿ 🖑O 🚲 DRY 👣 Some
rooms en-suite
♈ 10 £5/person ⛺ 2 £5/person 🗎 🐴
🐴 🕭 🗎 🚲 DRY
🌙 4 £12 ☀ 4 £12
🍴 Horsebox parking available for guests

INN | **Inn with the Well**

Mr Mike Shaw
Marlborough Road, Ogbourne St
George, Marlborough SN8 1SQ
T: 01672 841445 **F:** 01672 841056
E: info@theinnwiththewell.com
www.theinnwiththewell.co.uk
🛏 3 £55 🛏 2 £55 (£45) 🛏 1 £75
⚥ ♿ 🗎 V ♿ 🖑 🌙 🚲 DRY 👣 💳
Most major cards ★★★ All rooms
en-suite

Lower Herdswick Farm   **B&B** ♈

Mrs Jemima Milton
Ogbourne St George, Marlborough SN8
1SY
T: 01672 841166 **F:** 01672 841120
M: 07866 529128
E: jemimamilton@btinternet.com
www.herdswick.co.uk
🛏 2 £55 🛏 1 £55 (£40) ⚥ 🗎 V
🖑 🚲 DRY 🚗 👣
🌙 5 £10 ☀ 5 £8
🍴 Horsebox parking available for guests

Ogbourne St George

Racehorses on gallops at Kingston Lisle

Strip lynchet, Bishopstone

Section 2

Ogbourne St George
to Sparsholt Firs

Probably the most remote section of The Ridgeway, this 16 miles (25.6km)
runs along the scarp face of the downs passing two Iron Age forts at
Liddington and Uffington, the Stone Age long barrow of Wayland's Smithy
and the wonderful figure of the Uffington White Horse. It also passes
the only pub, at Fox Hill, directly on the western half of the Trail!

(Not to scale)

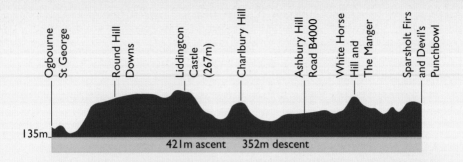

Ogbourne St George — Round Hill Downs — Liddington Castle (267m) — Charlbury Hill — Ashbury Hill Road B4000 — White Horse Hill and The Manger — Sparsholt Firs and Devil's Punchbowl

135m

421m ascent   352m descent

Maps

Landranger maps	174	Newbury and Wantage
Explorer maps	157	Marlborough and Savernake Forest
	170	Abingdon, Wantage and Vale of White Horse

Taxis

Place	Name	Telephone Number
Lambourn	Ray's	01488 71819
Childrey	Berkely Executive Cars	07775 647790
East Challow	Bonny's Taxis	07753 165890
	Grove Cabs	01235 772200
Letcombe Regis	Regis Cars of Wantage	07748 183381
Wantage	Cab Co	01235 772424
	Chapel Cars	07789 551931
	Evenlode Taxis	01235 762035
	Keith's of Wantage	01235 763344
	Stuart's Taxis	01235 770608
	Webb's of Wantage	07881 647777

Car Parking

If you choose to park in villages close to The Ridgeway, please park considerately. Other places to park are listed below but you need to be aware that theft from cars parked in the countryside does occur. You are advised to leave any unnecessary items at home or, failing that, ensure that anything valuable is locked in the boot of your vehicle.

Place	Map Grid Reference
On Ridgeway at Fox Hill near Wanborough, 200m north-east of Shepherds Rest pub on road to Hinton Parva	SU 233814
On Ridgeway 1/2 mile (1km) south of Ashbury on B4000	SU 274844
National Trust car park for Uffington White Horse, south off B4507, 1/2 mile (700m) north of The Ridgeway	SU 293866
On Ridgeway at Sparsholt Firs on the south side of B4001, 21/2 miles (4km) south of Childrey	SU 344851

Water Points

* with troughs for animals

Place	Map Grid Reference
Elm Tree Cottage, Southend	SU 198734
Idstone Barn, Ashbury*	SU 263835
Hill Barn, Sparsholt Firs*	SU 338854

Toilets

Place	Map Grid Reference
Shepherds Rest Pub, Fox Hill (patrons only)	SU 232813

Vets

* large animal vets

Place	Name	Telephone Number
Swindon	Eastcott Veterinary Hospital	01793 528341
	The Drove Veterinary Hospital	01793 522483
	Thameswood Veterinary Clinic	01793 511267
Lambourn	Mildenhall Veterinary Centre	01488 72900
	Ridgeway Veterinary Clinic	01488 71505
	Ridgeway Veterinary Group*	01488 71999
Faringdon	Danetree Veterinary Surgeons	01367 242777
	Elms Veterinary Surgery	01367 242416
Stanford in the Vale	Christoper Day	01367 710324
(near Faringdon)	(Alternative Therapies)	
Wantage	Abivale Veterinary Group	01235 770333
	Danetree Veterinary Surgeons	01235 770227

Farriers

Place	Name	Telephone Number
Uffington	Mervyn Richings	01367 820253
Lambourn	AVR Campbell	07702 126620
	LA Cartmell	01488 71985
	Chapel Forge Farriers	01488 72613
	AJ Charles	01488 71310
	A K Eadie	07818 886806
	M L Franks	07990 823481
	Micheal Jones	01488 72848
	SL King	07798 836205

43

Saddlers

Place	Name	Telephone Number
Lambourn	E J Wicks	01488 71766
Faringdon	Horse Shoe Saddlery	01367 710797
Kingston Lisle	Bowlby Equine	01367 820888
Childrey	White Horse Animal Feeds	01235 751529

Riding Stables for Guided Rides

Place	Name	Telephone Number
Lambourn	Folly Foot Stables	01488 658585
Kingston Lisle	Holistic Horses	01367 820033

Horsebox Parking

The following places have sufficient space for you to park your horsebox. You **must** call in advance to arrange as space may be scarce. A fee may also be charged.

Place	Name	Telephone Number
Bishopstone	Royal Oak Free for day-riders	01793 790481
Sparsholt	Down Barn Farm (Accommodation guests and day-riders)	01367 820272

Bike Repairs

Place	Name	Telephone Number
Swindon	Mitchell Cycles	01793 523306
	Swindon Cycles Superstore	01793 700105
	Bike Doctor	01793 874873
	Total Bike	01793 644185
Wantage	Ridgeway Cycles	01235 764445
	GMC	01235 764204

Mountain Bike Hire

Place	Name	Telephone Number
Swindon	Swindon Cycles Superstore (local delivery and car rack hire)	01793 700105

Tourist Information Centres

These TICs are staffed but note that many libraries in the area have leaflets about local attractions and events.

★ offers accommodation booking service

Place	Address/Opening Hours
★ Swindon	37 Regent Street, Swindon SN1 1JL **T**: 01793 530328 **F**: 01793 434031 **E**: infocentre@swindon.gov.uk **W**: www.visitswindon.co.uk Opening hours: All year: Mon-Sat 09:15-17:00
★ Faringdon	The Pump House, 5 Market Place, Faringdon SN7 7HL **T/F**: 01367 242191 **E**: tourism@faringdontowncouncil.org.uk **W**: www.whitehorsedc.gov.uk Opening hours: Summer (1 Apr-31 Oct) Mon-Fri 9:30-16:30, Sat 9:30-13:00 Winter (1 Nov-31 Mar) Mon-Sat 10:00-13:00
★ Wantage	Vale and Downland Museum & Visitor Centre 19 Church Street, Wantage OX12 8BL **T**: 01235 771447 **F**: 01235 760991 **E**: museum@wantage.com **W**: www.wantage.com/museum Opening hours: All year: Mon-Sat 10:30-16:30

Uffington Castle

ALDBOURNE

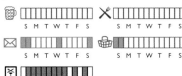

SU2675 3.3 miles (5.2km)
Swindon 10 miles (16km)
&WC

S M T W T F S   S M T W T F S

S M T W T F S   S M T W T F S

S M T W T F S

in Post Office and Co-Op

Crown at Aldbourne

Mr Geoff Eccleston
The Square, Aldbourne, Marlborough
SN8 2DU
T: 01672 540214 **M:** 07808 914552
F: 01672 541050 **E:** enquiries@
crownataldbourne.co.uk
www.crownataldbourne.co.uk
4 £70 1 £70 (£50)
V Most major cards ★★★★
All rooms en-suite

LIDDINGTON

SU2081 0.6 miles (1km)
Swindon 4 miles (7km)

S M T W T F S   S M T W T F S

Pubs: Sun 01793 790262 & Village Inn
01793 790314

☆ Liddington Castle
www.themodernantiquarian.com/site/3080

WANBOROUGH

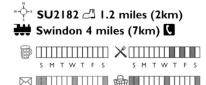

SU2182 1.2 miles (2km)
Swindon 4 miles (7km)

S M T W T F S   S M T W T F S

S M T W T F S   S M T W T F S

in Post Office

Garden Apartment   SC

Mrs Julie Evans
The Bungalow, Chapel Lane,
Wanborough, Swindon SN4 0AJ
T: 01793 791395 **M:** 07973 322163
E: tom.m.evans@talk21.com
www.swindonaccommodation.co.uk
Prices from £240 ★★★

BISHOPSTONE

SU2483 0.6 miles (1km)
Swindon 7 miles (11km)

S M T W T F S   S M T W T F S

Pubs: Royal Oak 01793 790481 & True
Heart 01793 790080

Cheney Thatch   *closed Xmas* B&B

Mrs R D Boot
Oxon Place, Bishopstone, Swindon
SN6 8PS
T: 01793 790508
2 £50 (£40) (over 9) V O
★★★ All rooms en-suite

B&B | **Prebendal Farm** *closed Xmas & New Year*

Mrs Jo Selbourne
Bishopstone, Swindon SN6 8PT
T: 01793 790485 **F:** 01793 791487
E: prebendal@aol.com
www.prebendal.com
🛏 3 £70 ⬦ 1 £70 (£35) ✨ 🔲 V
🔥 ⓘ O 🚲🚗 🚶 Some rooms en-suite

Cheney Thatch

Bishopstone, Swindon, Wiltshire
Tel 01793 790508

16th Century stone thatched cottage
in unique peaceful setting.
Trout stream through garden,
summer marquee. Heated outdoor
swimming pool. Footpath to
Ridgeway from garden gate.

Royal Oak 🏠

Mr Mark Genders
Cues Lane, Bishopstone, Swindon
SN6 8PP
T: 01793 790481 **F:** 01793 791239
M: 07988 719689
E: royaloak@helenbrowningorganics.
co.uk
www.helenbrowningorganics.co.uk
🛏 2 £60 ⬦ 1 £60 (£35) ✨ 🔲 V
🔥 🍷🍎● 🚲 🗂 🚗 🚶 💳 Most
major cards.
🍴 Most food provided is grown on our
own organic farm.

ASHBURY

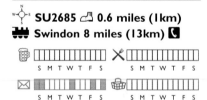

🧭 **SU2685** 👢 **0.6 miles (1km)**
🚂 **Swindon 8 miles (13km)** 📞

Pub: Rose & Crown Hotel 01793
710222

☆ Ashdown House
T: 01793 762209
www.nationaltrust.org.uk

B&B | **Ashbury Stores** *closed Xmas & New Year*

Mrs Jean-Anne Schiff
2 High Street, Ashbury, Swindon
SN6 8NA
T: 01793 710262
E: jeananneschiff@yahoo.co.uk
🛏 I £60 🛏 I £60 (£35) ♀♀(over 4)
V 🌰 🌶 🍎 O 🚲 **DRY** 🥾
🍴 Private bathroom available

INN | **Rose & Crown**

Mr Keith Walkley-Pratt
The High Street, Ashbury, Swindon
SN6 8NA
T: 01793 710222 **F:** 01793 710798
www.swindonweb.com
🛏 3 £60 🛏 3 £60 (£40) 🛏 I £40
♀♀ V 🌰 🌶 🍎 🚲 🚗 🥾 **VISA** Most
major cards. All rooms en-suite

WOOLSTONE

⊕ **SU2987** 🥾 I.2 miles (2km)
🚂 Swindon II miles (18km)

🍺 ▯▯▯▯▯▯▯▯▯ ✕ ▯▯▯▯▯▯▯▯▯
　　S M T W T F S　　　S M T W T F S
Pub: White Horse Inn 01367 820726

Blackthorn

White Horse | **INN**

Mr Angus Tucker
Woolstone, Faringdon SN7 7QL
T: 01367 820726 **F:** 01367 820566
www.whitehorsewoolstone.co.uk
🛏 3 £70 🛏 2 £70 🛏 I £70 ♀♀
♿ 🌰 V 🌰 🌶 🍎 🚲 🚗 🥾 **VISA**
Most major cards ★★★ Some rooms
en-suite

UFFINGTON

⊕ **SU3089** 🥾 I.9 miles (3km)
🚂 Swindon I2 miles (19km) 📞

　　S M T W T F S　　　S M T W T F S

　　S M T W T F S　　　S M T W T F S

🍵 ▯▯▯▯▯▯▯▯▯ Open summer only
　　S M T W T F S

Pub: Fox & Hounds 01367 820680
☆ Tom Brown's School Museum
T: 01367 820259 www.tombrown.
btinternet.co.uk/museum/index.html

☆ Uffington White Horse and Castle
T: 01793 762209
www.nationaltrust.org.uk

Norton House *closed Xmas* **B&B**

Mrs Fenella Oberman
Broad Street, Uffington, Faringdon SN7
7RA
T/F: 01367 820230
E: carloberman@aol.com
🛏 I £55 🛏 I £55 🛏 I £80 (£40)
🛏 I £30 ♀♀ 🌰 V 🌰 🍎 O 🚲 **DRY** 🍳
🚗 🥾 ★★★★
🍴 Private bathroom available

Britchcombe Countryside Holidays

Mrs M E A Seymour
Britchcombe Farm, Uffington, Faringdon
SN7 7QJ
T: 01367 820667 **M:** 07748 005362
F: 01367 821022 **E:** marcella@
seymour8227.freeserve.co.uk
 30 £6/person 20 £6/person

B&B | **Craven**

Mrs Carol Wadsworth
Fernham Road, Uffington, Faringdon
SN7 7RD
T: 01367 820449 **M:** 07771 567016
E: carol@thecraven.co.uk
www.thecraven.co.uk
3 £70 (£35)
Most major cards. All rooms en-suite

KINGSTON LISLE

SU3287 1.2 miles (2km)
Swindon 14 miles (22km)

S M T W T F S   S M T W T F S

Pub: Blowingstone Inn 01367 820288

Blowingstone Inn

Mr Nick Bishop
Kingston Lisle, Wantage OX12 9QL
T/F: 01367 820288
E: info@theblowingstone.co.uk
www.theblowingstone.co.uk
2 £60 1 £60 (£40) 2 £30
Most major cards ★★★★ All rooms en-suite

Blowingstone Inn

Kingstone Lisle, Wantage
Tel 01367 820288

We are located at the foot of
Blowingstone Hill, less than 2 miles
from the White Horse of Uffington
in the beautiful village of Kingston
Lisle. We look forward to offering you
a warm friendly welcome, good food,
fine wines & ales, lovely gardens in
summer - cosy log fires in winter.

SPARSHOLT

⊕ **SU3487** ⌁ **1.9 miles (3km)**

🚆 **Didcot 12 miles (20km)** 📞

▦ 𝕀𝕀𝕀𝕀𝕀𝕀𝕀𝕀𝕀𝕀𝕀𝕀 ✕ ▮𝕀𝕀𝕀𝕀𝕀𝕀𝕀𝕀𝕀
   S M T W T F S   S M T W T F S

Pub: Star Inn 01235 751539

B&B | **Westcot Lodge** | *closed Xmas*

Mrs P Upton
Westcot, Wantage OX12 9QA
T/F: 01235 751251 **M:** 07730 124888
🛏 1 £70 🛏 1 £70 (£40) 🛏 1 £35
⚥ V 🚶 🚲 **DRY** 🔘 🚗 🐾
Some rooms en-suite
☝ Private bathroom available

Down Barn Farm | *closed Xmas* | **B&B**
⚥ ∪

Mrs Penny Reid
Sparsholt Down , Wantage OX12 9XD
T: 01367 820272 **M:** 07799 833115
E: pendomeffect@aol.com
🛏 1 £60 🛏 2 £50 (£35) ⚥ ♿ 🖼
V 🚶 🌙 🚲 **DRY** 🔘 🚗 🐾 ★★★
Some rooms en-suite
⛺ 3 £5/person ☎ 1 £20 🔲 🔧 🔧 🚻
🔲 🚲 **DRY** 🔘
Ⓢ 4 £15 ⊕ 8 £5
☝ Down Barn is an organic farm.
Evening meals not available every
Sunday. Call in advance to arrange
horsebox parking for guests and day-
riders

Roden Downs, north of Compton

Section 3

Sparsholt Firs to Streatley

This 17.4 miles (27.9km) stretch keeps to the high scarp edge before losing height towards the end as it drops into the Thames Valley. It includes the widest parts of the Trail and some of the best conditions underfoot. This is racehorse country with gallops alongside the Trail in many places.

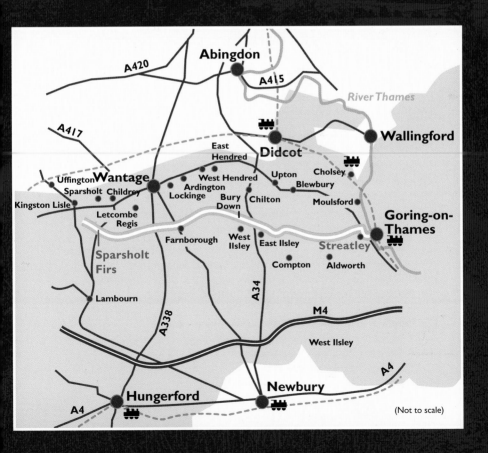

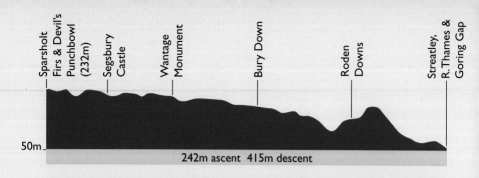

50m

242m ascent 415m descent

Maps

| Landranger maps | 174 | Newbury and Wantage |
| Explorer maps | 170 | Abingdon, Wantage and Vale of White Horse |

Taxis

Place	Name	Telephone Number
Childrey	Berkely Executive Cars	07775 647790
East Challow	Grove Cabs	01235 772200
Letcombe Regis	Regis Cars of Wantage	07748 183381
Wantage	Cab Co	01235 772424
	Chapel Cars	07789 551931
	Evenlode Taxis	01235 762035
	Keith's of Wantage	01235 763344
	Stuart's Taxis	01235 770608
	Webb's of Wantage	07881 647777
Aston Upthorpe	Astons Airport Services	07837 343680

Car Parking

If you choose to park in villages close to The Ridgeway, please park considerately. Other places to park are listed below but you need to be aware that theft from cars parked in the countryside does occur. You are advised to leave any unnecessary items at home or, failing that, ensure that anything valuable is locked in the boot of your vehicle.

Place	Map Grid Reference
On Ridgeway at Sparsholt Firs on the south side of B4001, 2¹/2 miles (4km) south of Childrey	SU 344851
On Ridgeway on the east side of B4494, 3 miles (5km) south of Wantage	SU 417843
On Ridgeway at Scutchamer's Knob, 2 miles (3km) south of East Hendred off the A417 east of Wantage	SU 458851
On Ridgeway at Bury Down on minor road from A34 to West Ilsley (signed Ridgeway from A34)	SU 479841
On Ridgeway at end of Rectory Road, Streatley, west off A417	SU 567813

Water Points

* with troughs for animals

Place	Map Grid Reference
Hill Barn, Sparsholt Firs*	SU 338854
The Court Hill Ridgeway Centre (YHA), Letcombe Regis*	SU 393849

Toilets

Place	Map Grid Reference
The Court Hill Ridgeway Centre (YHA), Letcombe Regis	SU 393849

Vets

* large animal vets

Place	Name	Telephone Number
Lambourn	Mildenhall Veterinary Centre	01488 72900
	Ridgeway Veterinary Clinic	01488 71505
	Ridgeway Veterinary Group*	01488 71999
Stanford in the Vale (near Faringdon)	Christoper Day (Alternative Therapies)	01367 710324
Wantage	Abivale Veterinary Group	01235 511533
	Danetree Veterinary Surgeons	01235 770227
West Ilsley	The Cottages Veterinary Surgery	01635 281344
Goring-on-Thames	The Goring Veterinary Centre	01491 873638

Farriers

Place	Name	Telephone Number
Wantage	GP Feltham	07768 637068
	RGD Godfrey	01235 868492
	TM Webb	01235 765307
Blewbury	Ian Belcher	01235 850029
	Phillippa Jeffries	07887 574112

After harvest near Streatley

Saddlers

Place	Name	Telephone Number
Denchworth	Denchworth Equestrian Supplies	01235 868175
Blewbury	Equestrain UK Ltd	01235 851177
	Stable Door Saddlery	01235 850725

Riding Stables for Guided Riding

Place	Name	Telephone Number
Kingston Lisle	Holistic Horses	01367 820033
Blewbury	Blewbury Riding & Training Centre	01235 851016

Horsebox Parking

The following places have sufficient space for you to park your horsebox. You **must** call in advance to arrange as space may be scarce. A fee may also be charged.

Place	Name	Telephone Number
Lockinge	Lockinge Kiln Farm (Accommodation guests and day-riders)	01235 763308
Blewbury	The Red Lion (Accommodation guests and day-riders free parking)	01235 850403
Streatley	Linden Cottage (Accommodation guests and day-riders)	01491 871120

Bike Repairs

Place	Name	Telephone Number
Wantage	Ridgeway Cycles	01235 764445
	GMC	01235 764204
Abingdon	Behind Bars Cycle Shop	01235 533287
	Pedal Power	01235 525123
	Rides on Air	01235 555571
Moulsford	Trail Junkies MBT Centre	01993 842396
Pangbourne	Mountain High	0118 9841851

Mountain Bike Hire

Place	Name	Telephone Number
Abingdon	Pedal Power	01235 525123
Moulsford	Trail Junkies MBT Centre	01993 842396
Pangbourne	Mountain High	0118 9841851

Tourist Information Centres

These TICs are staffed but note that many libraries in the area have leaflets about local attractions and events.

★ offers accommodation booking service

Place	Address/Opening Hours
★ Wantage	Vale and Downland Museum & Visitor Centre 19 Church Street, Wantage OX12 8BL **T**: 01235 771447 **F**: 01235 760991 **E**: museum@wantage.com **W**: www.wantage.com/museum Opening hours: All year: Mon-Sat 10:30-16:30
Abingdon	Visitor information Point, Old Abbey House, Abbey Close, Abingdon OX14 3JD **T**: 01235 522711 **F**: 01235 533112 **E**: townclerk@abingdon.gov.uk **W**: www.abingdon.gov.uk Opening hours: Mon-Fri 09:00-17:00

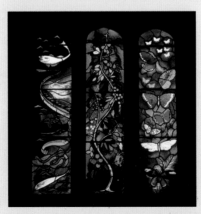

John Piper window in Farnborough church

55

LETCOMBE REGIS

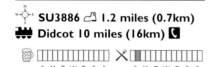

⌖ **SU3886** 🚶 **1.2 miles (0.7km)**
🚌 **Didcot 10 miles (16km)** 📞

🍺 |||||||||||| ✕ ▌|||||||||||
　 S M T W T F S 　 S M T W T F S

Pub: Greyhound Inn 01235 771093

B&B █ **9 Croft End**

Mrs Joyce Coombs
Letcombe Regis, Wantage OX12 9JJ
T: 01235 763694 **M:** 07770 580656
E: joyce.coombs@dsl.pipex.com
🛏 1 £60 🛏 1 £60 (£35) ✨ ♿ 💼
V 🏔 🍴 O 🚲 **DRY** 🅾 🚗 🔖 Some
rooms en-suite

B&B █ **Quince Cottage** *closed xmas & New Year*

Mrs Louise Boden
Letcombe Regis, Wantage OX12 9JP
T: 01235 763652 **M:** 07989 649680
E: bodens@supanet.com
www.rboden.supanet.com
🛏 1 £60 🛏 1 £80 (£35) ✨ V 🏔
🚲 **DRY** 🅾 🔖
◀ Private bathroom available

Greyhound Inn 🏨

Mr F Mahon
Main Street, Letcombe Regis, Wantage
OX12 9JL
T: 01235 771093 **F:** 01235 770905
E: greyhoundregis@aol.com
www. greyhound-inn.co.uk
🛏 2 £60 🛏 1 £60 🛏 1 £30/person
(£30) 🛏 2 £30 ✨ ♿ 💼 V 🏔 🍎 O
🚲 **DRY** 🅾 🚗 🔖 🚾 Most major
cards. Some rooms en-suite

Court Hill Centre *phone ahead* ▲ C ⛺

The Manager
Court Hill, Letcombe Regis, Wantage
OX12 9NE
T: 01235 760253
E: info@courthill.org.uk
www.courthill.org.uk
✨ ♿ V 🏔 O 🚲 **DRY** 🚾 Most
major cards.
▲ Several £6 🚰 🚿 ♿WC 🖥 🚲
DRY 🍳 CG
Ⓢ 4 £10
◀ Private and dormitory
accommodation available from £14/
adult. Tea rooms open daily April to
September, and Thursdays to Mondays
October to March.

**Riders on
The Ridgeway
above Wantage**

WANTAGE

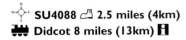 **SU4088** 2.5 miles (4km)

🚉 **Didcot 8 miles (13km)** ℹ

Town with full range of services, visit www.wantage.com for further details. It has a wide range of accommodation - details from Visitor Centre (see section introduction). Farmers Market last Saturday of each month.

☆ The Vale & Downland Museum **T**: 01235 771447 www.wantage.com/museum

LOCKINGE

SU4287 2.1 miles (3.4km)

🚉 **Didcot 7.5 miles (12km)** 📞

&B ∪ | **Lockinge Kiln Farm** *closed Xmas-March*
GR SU424834 0.6miles(1km) south of Ridgeway
Mrs Stella Cowan
The Ridgeway, Chain Hill, Wantage
OX12 8PA
T/F: 01235 763308
E: stellacowan@hotmail.com
www.lockingekiln.co.uk
🛏 1 £50 🛏 2 £50 (£30) 👫 (over 9)
V 🏍 🌑 ♦ 🚲 **DRY** 🔘 🐾
(S) 5 £11 🍴 6 £7
🍴 Evening meals not available on Fri Sat or Sun. Call in advance to arrange horsebox parking for day-riders.

Andersey Farm   SC

Mrs Janine Beaumont
Grove Park Drive, Lockinge, Wantage
OX12 8SG
T: 01235 771866
E: anderseyfarmt@googlemail.com
www.anderseyfarmcottage.co.uk
Self-catering cottage available from £250/week. ★★★★

Lockinge Kiln Farm

The Ridgeway, Wantage, Oxfordshire
Tel/Fax: 01235 763308

Comfortable farmhouse enjoying a quiet country location, just 1/2 mile south of The Ridgeway. Ideal walking / cycling/horseriding.

ARDINGTON

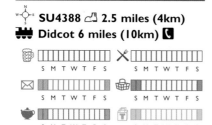 SU4388 ⌂ 2.5 miles (4km)
🚂 Didcot 6 miles (10km) 📞

	S M T W T F S		S M T W T F S
🍺	ⅢⅢⅢⅢⅢ	✕	ⅢⅢⅢⅢⅢ
✉	ⅢⅢⅢⅢⅢ	🧺	ⅢⅢⅢⅢⅢ
🍵	ⅢⅢⅢⅢⅢ	🏪	ⅢⅢⅢⅢⅢ

Pub: Boar's Head 01235 833254

FARNBOROUGH

 SU4382 ⌂ 1.8 miles (2.9km)
🚂 Newbury 11.3 miles (18km)

☆ John Betjeman memorial window by John Piper in church

B&B ◡ **Old Smithy**

Mrs Lorna Gwinner
Farnborough, Wantage OX12 8NX
T: 01488 638782 **F:** 01488 638092
E: angus@wordsmith-ltd.com
🛏 1 £55 🛏 1 £55 (£35) 📺 V 🚶
🚲 DRY 🗒 🚗
H Stabling for horses can be arranged in advance with neighbour. Transport available to pub for evening meal.

WEST HENDRED

 SU4488 ⌂ 2.5 miles (4km)
🚂 Didcot 6 miles (9km) 📞

	S M T W T F S		S M T W T F S
🍺	ⅢⅢⅢⅢⅢ	✕	ⅢⅢⅢⅢⅢ

Pub: Hare 01235 833249

EAST HENDRED

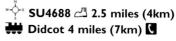 SU4688 ⌂ 2.5 miles (4km)
🚂 Didcot 4 miles (7km) 📞

	S M T W T F S		S M T W T F S
🍺	ⅢⅢⅢⅢⅢ	✕	ⅢⅢⅢⅢⅢ
✉	ⅢⅢⅢⅢⅢ	🧺	ⅢⅢⅢⅢⅢ

☆ Champs Chapel Museum - Open Sundays only (limited opening Oct - Mar) T: 01235 833312 www.hendred.org/champs.htm

☆ Hendred Vineyard T: 01235 820081 www.hendredvineyard.co.uk

Monk's Court B&B

Mrs Susie Turnbull
Newbury Road, East Hendred, Wantage OX12 8LG
T: 01235 833797 **M:** 07710 274653
F: 01235 862554
E: susieturnbull@monkscourt.co.uk
www.monkscourt.co.uk
🛏 2 £65 🛏 1 £65 (£35) ⚶ 📺 V
🚶 🍴 🚲 DRY 🗒 🚗 ★★★ Some rooms en-suite; other has private bathroom.

B&B **Cowdrays** *closed Xmas & Easter*

Mrs Margaret Bateman
Cat Street, East Hendred, Wantage
OX12 8JT
T: 01235 833313 **M:** 07799 622003
E: cowdrays@virgin.net
www.cowdrays.co.uk
🛏 2 £80 🛏 2 £70 (£35) 🛏 1 £35
🏃 ♿ 📷 V 🏔 🍴 🚲 DRY 🔲 🚗 🐾
★★★

B&B **Greensands Guest House**
SC

Ms Jane McCourt
Reading Road, East Hendred, Wantage
OX12 8JE
T: 01235 833338 **M:** 07884 002203
F: 01235 821632
E: janemccourt@aol.com
www.greensandsguesthouse.co.uk
🛏 5 £70 🛏 4 £70 🛏 2 £100
(£40) 🛏 1 £40 🏃 ♿ 📷 V 🏔 DRY 🔲
VISA Mastercard, Visa. All rooms en-suite
🏠 4 self catering chalets, £70/night

WEST ILSLEY

⊕ **SU4782** 1.2 miles (2km)
🚂 **Didcot 7 miles (11km)** 📞

🍺 |||||||||||| ✕ ||||||||||||
S M T W T F S   S M T W T F S

Pub: Harrow Inn 01635 281260

CHILTON

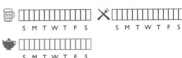

⊕ **SU4986** 1.2 miles (2km)
🚂 **Didcot 4 miles (6km) P F** 📞

🍺 |||||||||||| ✕ ||||||||||||
S M T W T F S   S M T W T F S

🫖 ||||||||||||
S M T W T F S

Pub: Rose & Crown 01235 862992

EAST ILSLEY

⊕ **SU4981** 1.2 miles (2km)
🚂 **Didcot 7 miles (11km)** 📞

🍺 |||||||||||| ✕ ||||||||||||
S M T W T F S   S M T W T F S

Crown & Horns Inn INN

Mrs Sally Allsop
The Square, East Ilsley RG20 7LH
T: 01635 281545 **F:** 0870 1312567
E: crownandhorns@btinternet.com
🛏 6 £70 🛏 1 £70 🛏 3 £75 (£60)
🏃 📷 V 🏔 🍴 🚲 VISA All major
cards. All rooms en-suite
🏠 Laundry and drying facilities by
arrangement

Harebells

Swan Hotel

Mr Richard Vellender
High St, East Ilsley RG20 7LF
T: 01635 281238
E: kimrichstar@aol.com
www.theswaneastilsley.co.uk

🛏 2 £75 🛏 3 £75 (£65) 🚼 (over
11) 🔌 V 🖾 🌑 🛈 🚲 DRY 🚗 🚶 VISA
Most major cards. All rooms en-suite
🍴 Evening meals not available Sundays

UPTON

🧭 **SU5186** 👢 **2.5 miles (4km)**
🚂 **Didcot 3 miles (5km)** 📞

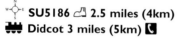
S M T W T F S   S M T W T F S

S M T W T F S

Pub: George & Dragon 01235 850723
(closed Sunday evenings winter only)

B&B � ### Prospect House

Mrs Hilary Powell
Upton, Didcot OX11 9HU
T: 01235 850268 **M:** 07966 205688
E: srjpowell@lineone.net

🛏 2 £65 🛏 1 £65 (£35) 🚼 V 🚲
DRY 🔲 ★★★★
🌀 2 £10

COMPTON

🧭 **SU5280** 👢 **1.2 miles (2km)**
🚂 **Goring 6 miles (9km) PF** 📞

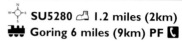
S M T W T F S   S M T W T F S

BLEWBURY

🧭 **SU5385** 👢 **2.5 miles (4km)**
🚂 **Didcot 4 miles (6km) PF** 📞

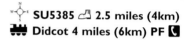
S M T W T F S   S M T W T F S

S M T W T F S

Red Lion   🏨

Stuart Mace & Peter Matthews
Chapel Lane, Blewbury OX11 9PQ
T: 01235 850403 **F:** 01235 850666
E: enquiries@redlionblewbury.co.uk
www.redlionblewbury.co.uk

🛏 1 £50 🛏 1 £50 🛏 1 £60 (£50)
🛏 1 £50 🚼 🔌 V 🖾 🌑 🛈 O 🚲
DRY 🔲 🚆 VISA All major cards. All rooms
en-suite

Yew Tree   B&B

Mrs Liz Thacker
London Road, Blewbury OX11 9PF
T/F: 01235 850678
E: lizthackeryewtree@hotmail.com

🛏 1 £40 (£55) 🛏 1 £35 🚼 (over
11) V 🛈 🚲 DRY 🚗 🚶 Some rooms
en-suite

Swan Hotel

East Ilsley
Tel 01635 281238

Traditional 17th century inn, recently refurbished with 5 en-suite
bedrooms including a magnificent four-poster suite.
Previously licencees at The Star, East Ilsley, Richard and Kim
have been welcoming users of The Ridgeway for the last six years
and look forward to welcoming you to the Swan.

For further information please view our website at www.theswaneastilsley.co.uk
For reservations please phone 01635 281238

ALDWORTH

SU5579 👞 1.2 miles (2km)
🚆 **Goring 3 miles (5km)** 📞

🍺 ‖‖‖‖‖‖‖‖‖ ✗‖‖‖‖‖‖‖‖‖
  S M T W T F S   S M T W T F S
🧺 ‖‖‖‖‖‖‖‖‖ 🫖‖‖‖‖‖‖‖‖‖
  S M T W T F S   S M T W T F S

Pubs: Bell 01635 578272 & Four Points
01635 578367

B&B **Fieldview Cottage**   *closed Xmas*

Mr & Mrs H Hunt
Bell Lane, Aldworth, Reading RG8 9SB
T: 01635 578964 **E:** hunt@fieldvu.
freeserve.co.uk
🛏 1 £60 🛏 1 £60 (£30) 🛏 1 £30
♿ **V** 🚲 **DRY** ★★★★

MOULSFORD

SU5983 👞 1.2 miles (2km)
🚆 **Cholsey 2 miles (3km)** 📞

🍺 ‖‖‖‖‖‖‖‖‖ ✗‖‖‖‖‖‖‖‖‖
  S M T W T F S   S M T W T F S
🧺 ‖‖‖‖‖‖‖‖‖
  S M T W T F S

Pub: Beetle & Wedge 01491 651381

Beetle & Wedge Boathouse   B&B

Ms Stephanie Hicks
Ferry Lane, Moulsford OX10 9JF
T: 01491 651381 **F:** 01491 651376
E: boathouse@beetleandwedge.co.uk
www. beetleandwedge.co.uk
🛏 3 £90 (£75) 👫 **V** 🚲 ⚫ 🍴 🍺
🚲 **DRY** 📺 🚗 🐾 VISA All major
cards. All rooms en-suite
⚑ 2 rooms can be twin if required

STREATLEY

SU5980 👞 on path
🚆 **Goring & Streatley 0.5 miles
(1km)** 📞

🍺 ‖‖‖‖‖‖‖‖‖ ✗‖‖‖‖‖‖‖‖‖
  S M T W T F S   S M T W T F S

Pubs: Swan at Streatley 01491 878800 &
Bull 01491 872392

☆ The Holies Nature Reserve
T: 0118 984 3040 www.nationaltrust.
org.uk

☆ Basildon Park
T: 0118 984 3040
www.nationaltrust.org.uk

☆ Beale Wildlife Park
T: 0870 777 7160
www.bealepark.co.uk

🏠 Swan at Streatley

Mr Karl Bentley
Streatley RG8 9HR
T: 01491 878800 **F:** 01491 872554
E: sales@swan-at-streatley.co.uk
www.swanatstreatley.co.uk
🛏 27 £105 🛏 9 £105 🛏 3 £135
(£90) 🛏 8 £80 ♦♦ ♿ ▣ V ◭ ◉ ◉ 🔥
▨ All major cards ★★★★ All rooms
en-suite

🏠 Bull at Streatley

Mrs A J Booker
Reading Road, Streatley RG8 9JJ
T: 01491 872392 **F:** 01491 875231
E: bull@inntownpub.com
www.thebullatstreatley.com
🛏 6 £70 (£70) ♦♦ ▣ V ◭ ◉ ◉◉
▨ All major cards ★★★ All rooms
en-suite
♦ One room can be twin at £100

▲ YHA Streatley   *closed Nov-Feb*

Mr Nick Crivich
Hill House, Reading Road, Streatley
RG8 9JJ
T: 01491 872278 **F:** 01491 873056
E: streatley@yha.org.uk
www.yhastreatley.org.uk
🛏 2 £40 🛏 8 £45 ♦♦ (over 1) V ◭
◉ ◉ ◉◉ DRY 🔥 ▨ Most major
cards ★★★ Some rooms en-suite
♦ Self-catering accommodation from
£17.95/unit

3 Ickneild Cottages   B&B

Mrs Susan Brodie
3 Ickneild Cottages, High Street,
Streatley RG8 9JA
T: 01491 875152 **M:** 07989 152295
F: 01491 875650
🛏 1 £30 V ◭ ◉ ◉ ◉◉ DRY ◉

Linden Cottage *closed Xmas & New Year* SC ◡

Mrs Sue Jubb
Streatley RG8 9NB
T: 01491 871120
E: lyndoncottage@dsl.pipex.com
www.lyndoncottage.dsl.pipex.com
☺ 2 £15/week
Self-catering cottage, sleeps 4 from
£225/week. Children welcome, no
smoking.
♦ Horsebox parking available for guests
and day-riders (latter charged £3/day)

Stable Cottages   B&B ◡

Mrs Diana Fenton
Wallingford Road, Streatley RG8 9JX
T: 01491 874408
🛏 1 £50 (£25) 🛏 1 £25 ♦♦ (over 9)
V ◭ ◉ ◉ ◉◉ DRY ◉ 🔥
☺ 2 £10

Grim's Ditch

St Botolph's, Swyncombe, early Norman church dedicated to the patron saint of travellers

Section 4

Streatley to Watlington

At the start of this 15.3 miles (24.6km) section The Ridgeway crosses another National Trail, the Thames Path, before following the bank of the River Thames for a few picturesque miles. The Trail then heads east into the more wooded Chilterns via an ancient Grim's Ditch and finishes on the wide track of the old Icknield Way.

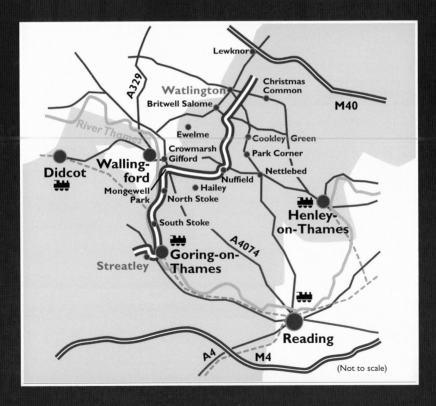

(Not to scale)

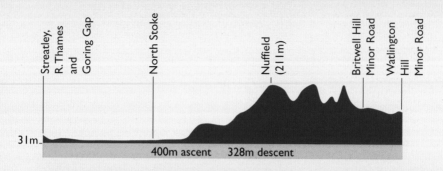

Maps

Landranger maps	174	Newbery and Wantage
	175	Reading and Windsor
Explorer maps	171	Chiltern Hills West

Taxis

Place	Name	Telephone Number
Goring-on-Thames	Airpal Taxis	07862 721698
	Golden Taxis	01491 871111
	Murdocks Taxis	01491 872029
Wallingford	Hills Taxis	01491 837022
Ipsden	Ipsden Private Hire	01491 680863
Nettlebed	David Byers of Nettlebed	01491 641159
Ewelme	Busher's Taxis	01491 826161

Car Parking

If you choose to park in villages close to The Ridgeway, please park considerately. Other places to park are listed below but you need to be aware that theft from cars parked in the countryside does occur. You are advised to leave any unnecessary items at home or, failing that, ensure that anything valuable is locked in the boot of your vehicle.

Place	Map Grid Reference
Goring-on-Thames public car park	SU 599807
On Ridgeway on west side of minor road, 1 mile (1½km) from Britwell Salome heading southeast	SU 681922
On Ridgeway on east side of Hill Road, minor road to Christmas Common ½ mile (1km) southeast of Watlington	SU 698940

Water Points

Place	Map Grid Reference
Grimsdyke Cottage, Grim's Ditch	SU 660872
Church, Nuffield (on the wall)	SU 667874
White Mark Farm Camp Site, Watlington (March – October)	SU 697939

Toilets

Place	Map Grid Reference
Goring-on-Thames (Car Park off Station Road)	SU 602807
White Mark Farm Camp Site, Watlington (March - October)	SU 697939
Watlington (High Street) ♿	SU 689945

Vets

Place	Name	Telephone Number
Goring-on-Thames	The Goring Veterinary Centre	01491 873638
Cholsey	Larkmead Veterinary Group	01491 651379
Wallingford	White TD & Stewart JD	01491 839043
Watlington	Crossroads Veterinary Centre	01491 612799

Farriers

Place	Name	Telephone Number
Watlington	William Smith	01491 612872
	Adrian Spilsbury	07968 065991

Saddlers

Place	Name	Telephone Number
Blewbury	Stable Door Saddlery	01235 850725
	Equestrian UK Ltd	01235 851016
Watlington	Cowboy Magic	01491 614960

Bike Repairs

Place	Name	Telephone Number
Moulsford	Trail Junkies MBT Centre	01993 842396
Pangbourne	Mountain High	0118 984 1851
Wallingford	Rides on Air	01491 836289

Mountain Bike Hire

Place	Name	Telephone Number
Abingdon	Pedal Power	01235 525123
Moulsford	Trail Junkies MBT Centre	01993 842396
Pangbourne	Mountain High	0118 984 1851

67

Tourist Information Centres

This TIC is staffed but note that many libraries in the area have leaflets about local attractions and events.

Place	Address/Opening Hours
Wallingford	Wallingford TIC, Town Hall, Market Place, Wallingford OX10 0EG
	T: 01491 826972 **F**: 01491 832925
	W: www.sodc.com
	Opening hours: Call in advance to check

View over Goring-on-Thames

GORING-ON-THAMES

⊕ **SU6080** 👢 **on path**

🚆 **Goring & Streatley** P**£** 📞 (♿)

♿WC

🍺	S M T W T F S	✕	S M T W T F S
✉	S M T W T F S	🧺	S M T W T F S
☕	S M T W T F S	🎬	S M T W T F S
🏧	S M T W T F S		

£ HSBC 🏧, Lloyds TSB

🛏 John Barleycorn

Mr G Reilly

Manor Road, Goring-on-Thames RG8
9DP

T: 01491 872509 **E:** enquiries@
thejohnbarleycornpub.co.uk
www.thejohnbarleycornpub.co.uk

🛏 3 £65 (£50) 👫 V 🏕 🌑 🍴 O
🚲 🔟 🚗 🐾 💳 Most major cards
★★★★ All rooms en-suite

B&B Melrose Cottage

Mrs Rosemary Howarth

36 Milldown Road, Goring-on-Thames
RG8 0BD

T: 01491 873040 **M:** 07798 663897

🛏 2 £50 (£30) 🛏 1 £30 V 🏕 🌑
🚲 DRY 🔟 🐾

Northview House *closed Xmas & New Year* B&B

Mrs I Sheppard

Farm Road, Goring-on-Thames RG8
0AA

T: 01491 872184

E: hi@goring-on-thames.freeserve.co.uk

🛏 1 £50 🛏 1 £50 🛏 1 £65 (£30)
🛏 1 £30 👫 V 🏕 🍴 O 🚲 DRY 🔟

Queens Arms 🛏

Mr J Everied

Reading Road, Goring-on-Thames
RG8 0ER

T: 01491 872825

E: queensarms@tesco.net

🛏 1 £70 🛏 1 £70 (£40) 🛏 2 £40
👫 (over 9) V 🏕 🌑 🚲

South Stoke church

SOUTH STOKE

SU5983 ⌂ **on path**
🚆 **Goring & Streatley 2 miles (3km)** ☎

🍺 ▯▯▯▯▯▯▯▯▯▯▯ ✕▯▮▯▯▯▯▯▯▯▯▯
S M T W T F S   S M T W T F S

Pub: Perch & Pike 01491 872415

B&B **Oak Barn**

Mrs Vanessa Guiver
The Old Post Office, South Stoke,
Reading RG8 0JS
T: 01491 871872 **M:** 07889 757767
F: 01491 871873 **E:** info@oakbarn.org
www.oakbarn.org
🛏 1 £70 (£40) ⚤ V 🖊 🚭 ☕ ●
🚲 **DRY** ⬚ 🚗 🕴 Room is en-suite
H Can accommodate 3rd person by
arrangement

INN **Perch & Pike**

Mr Neil Dorsett
The Street, South Stoke, Reading RG8
0JS
T: 01491 872415 **M:** 07840 684787
F: 01491 871001
E: info@perchandpike.co.uk
www.perchandpike.co.uk
🛏 3 £80 ⛌ 1 £80 (£70) ⚤ V 🖊
🚭 🕴 **VISA** Most major cards. All rooms
en-suite

NORTH STOKE

SU6086 ⌂ **on path**
🚆 **Goring & Streatley 4 miles (6km)**

🍺 ▯▯▯▯▯▯▯▯▯▯▯ ✕▯▯▯▯▯▯▯▯▯▯▯
S M T W T F S   S M T W T F S

Pub: Springs Hotel 01491 836687

Springs Hotel & Golf Club 🏨

Mr George Briffa
Wallingford Road, North Stoke,
Wallingford OX10 6BE
T: 01491 836687
E: info@thespringshotel.com
www.thespringshotel.com
🛏 19 £95 ⛌ 10 £95 ⛌ 3 £95
(£85) ⚤ 🕴 V 🖊 🚭 🚲 **DRY** ⬚
🚗 **VISA** Most major cards ★★★ All
rooms en-suite
H Family room supplement of £15/child
(under 12)

CROWMARSH GIFFORD

SU6189 ⌂ **0.6 miles (1km)**
🚆 **Didcot 6 miles (10km)** ☎

🍺 ▯▯▯▯▯▯▯▯▯▯▯ ✕▯▯▯▯▯▯▯▯▯▯▯
S M T W T F S   S M T W T F S

✉ ▮▯▯▯▯▯▮▯▯▯▯ 🧺▯▯▯▯▯▯▯▯▯▯▯
S M T W T F S   S M T W T F S

🎁 ▯▯▯▯▯▯▯▯▯▯▯
S M T W T F S

Pubs: Queen's Head 01491 839857 &
Bell Inn (Hungry Horse) 01491 835324

☆ Riverside Park & Swimming Pool
T: 01491 835232

B&B **Little Gables**

Mr & Mrs Tony & Jill Reeves
166 Crowmarsh Hill, Wallingford
OX10 8BG
T: 01491 837834 **M:** 07860 148882
F: 01491 834426
E: jill@stayingaway.com
www.stayingaway.com
🛏 2 £60 🛏 2 £60 🛏 2 £75 (£45)
🛏 1 £45 ⚥ ♿ 📺 V 🥾 🌢 🚲 DRY 👣
★★★★ Some rooms en-suite

Bridge Villa Camping & Caravan Park *closed Jan*

Mr A Townsend
The Street, Crowmarsh Gifford,
Wallingford OX10 8HB
T: 01491 836860 **M:** 07710 452429
F: 01491 836793
E: bridge.villa@btinternet.com
⛺ Numerous £8 🚐 Numerous £14 🏕
🛁 🚿 ⓝ ♿WC 📺 📞 🚲 DRY 🎛
📖 CG 💳 Most major cards ★★★★

Riverside Park *closed Oct-mid April*

Mr David Corringham
The Street, Wallingford Bridge,
Crowmarsh Gifford, Wallingford
OX10 8EB
T: 01491 835232
E: info@soll-leisure.co.uk
www.soll-leisure.co.uk
⛺ or 🚐 18 £10 🛁 🚿 ⓝ ♿WC 📺

WALLINGFORD

🧭 **SU6089** 🥾 1.2 miles (2km)
🚆 **Cholsey 6 miles (9km)** 🚉

Town with full range of services, visit
www.wallingfordtown.co.uk for further
details. Farmers Market 3rd Tues and
5th Saturday of the month. Local
Producers Market every Sat.

☆ Wallingford Museum
T: 01491 835065
www.wallingfordmuseum.org.uk

☆ Wallingford Castle
www.berkshirehistory.com/castles/
wallingford_cast.html

George Hotel

Mr Oliver Round-Turner
High Street, Wallingford OX10 0BS
T: 01491 836665 **F:** 01491 825359
E: rooms@george-hotel-wallingford.
com
www.peelhotel.com
🛏 22 £110 🛏 8 £110 🛏 1 £140
(£90) 🛏 8 £75 🕐 ⚥ ♿ V 🥾 🌢 🚲
DRY 💳 Most major cards ★★★ All
rooms en-suite

52 Blackstone Road B&B

Mrs Enid Barnard
Wallingford OX10 8JL
T: 01491 839339
E: enid.barnard@google.com
🛏 1 £40 (£30) 🛏 1 £20 V 🥾 🚲 DRY

HAILEY

⊹ SU6485 🥾 1.4 miles (2.3km)

🚂 Cholsey 5.3 miles (8.5km)

🍺 ⠿⠿⠿⠿⠿⠿ S M T W T F S ✗ ⠿⠿⠿⠿⠿⠿ S M T W T F S

Pub: King William IV 01491 681845

NUFFIELD

⊹ SU6687 🥾 on path

🚂 Henley-on-Thames 7 miles (11km) 📞

🍺 ⠿⠿⠿⠿⠿⠿ S M T W T F S ✗ ⠿⠿⠿⠿⠿⠿ S M T W T F S

Pub: Crown Inn 01491 641335

☆ Nuffield Place
T: 01491 641224
www.nuffield-place.com

B&B **Mays Farm**

⊹ GR SU654885 1.3 miles (2.1km)
from Ridgeway
Mrs P Passmore
Ewelme, Wallingford OX10 6QF
T: 01491 641294 **F:** 01491 641191

🛏 1 £50 🛏 1 £56 🛏 1 £60 (£35)
🛏 1 £30 ♀♂ V 🖊 **DRY** 🚗 ★★★★
Some rooms en-suite

14 Bradley Road *closed Xmas & New Year* B&B

Ms Diana Chambers
Nuffield, Henley-on-Thames RG9 5SG
T/F: 01491 641359 **M:** 07974 548528
E: dianamc@waitrose.com
🛏 2 £60 🛏 1 £60 ♀♂ 📺 V 🖊
🚲 **DRY** 🖨 🐾

NETTLEBED

⊹ SU70787 🥾 2.9 miles (4.6km)

🚂 Henley-on-Thames 5.2 miles (8.4km) **P F** 📞

🍺 ⠿⠿⠿⠿⠿⠿ S M T W T F S ✗ ⠿⠿⠿⠿⠿⠿ S M T W T F S

✉ ⠿⠿⠿⠿⠿⠿ S M T W T F S 🧺 ⠿⠿⠿⠿⠿⠿ S M T W T F S

Pub: White Hart Hotel 01491 641245

Somerset B&B

Mrs Nan McDonnell
9 High Street, Nettlebed, Henley-on-Thames RG9 5DA
T: 01491 641710 **E:** johnmcd@
somerset75.wanadoo.co.uk
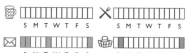
🛏 2 £52 (£26) ♀♂ (over 5) V 🚲
DRY 🚗 🐾 All rooms en-suite

EWELME

☼ **SU6491** 🥾 **1.3 miles (2.1km)**
🚂 **Henley-on-Thames 10.6 miles (17km) P F**

S M T W T F S   S M T W T F S

Pub: Shepherd's Hut 01491 835661

☆ Ewelme Watercress Beds
T: 01494 771250
www.chilternsociety.org.uk

B&B | **Fords Farm**

Miss M Edwards
Ewelme, Wallingford OX10 6HU
T: 01491 839272 **E:** fordsfarm@
callnetuk.com
www.fordsfarm.co.uk
🛏 1 £65 🛏 2 £65 (£45) **V** 🚲 🚴
DRY 🚗 🐾 ◆◆◆◆ Some rooms
en-suite
🎖 VisitBritain Silver Award.

Wild Rose

PARK CORNER

☼ **SU6988** 🥾 **1.2 miles (2km)**
🚂 **Henley-on-Thames 6 miles (10km)**

Park Corner Farmhouse **B&B** ☕

Mrs S M Rutter
Park Corner, Nettlebed, Henley-on-
Thames RG9 6DX
T: 01491 641450 **E:** parkcorner_
farmhouse@hotmail.com
🛏 2 £55 (£30) 🛏 1 £30 ✂ 📺 **V**🚴
🚲 🚗 🐾 ◆◆◆
㊉ 2 £10 ㊉ 4 £6

COOKLEY GREEN

☼ **SU6990** 🥾 **0.8 miles (1.2km)**
🚂 **Henley-on-Thames 7.5 miles (12km)** 📞

Pathways *closed Xmas* **B&B**

Mrs Ismayne Peters
Cookley Green, Swyncombe, Henley-
on-Thames RG9 6EN
T: 01491 641631 **E:** ismayne.peters@
tesco.net
🛏 1 £60 🛏 2 £60 (£35) ✂ (over
11) ♿ **V** 🚴 🍴 🚲 **DRY** 📺 🚗 🐾 All
rooms en-suite

BRITWELL SALOME

 **SU6787** 🥾 **0.6 miles (1km)**
🚉 **Henley-on-Thames 11 miles (17km)** ☎

🍺 |▮▮▮|||||||||| ✕ |▮||▮||||||||
  S M T W T F S   S M T W T F S

Pub: Goose 01491 61230

Walkers in the Chilterns

WATLINGTON

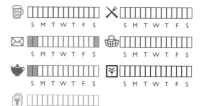 **SU6894** 🥾 **0.6 miles (1km)**
🚉 **Henley-on-Thames 10 miles (16km) P F** ☎ 🛈 ♿ WC

🍺 ||||||||||| ✕ |||||||||||
  S M T W T F S   S M T W T F S

✉ |▮||||||||| 🛒 |||||||||||
  S M T W T F S   S M T W T F S

☕ |▮||||||||| 🗟 |||||||||||
  S M T W T F S   S M T W T F S

⛽ |||||||||||
  S M T W T F S

£ Barclays, 🏧 in Co-Op
☆ Watlington Hill and White Mark
www.nationaltrust.org.uk

Woodgate Orchard Cottage   B&B

Ms Ronnie Roberts
Howe Road, Watlington OX49 5EL
T: 01491 612675
🛏 2 £50 🛏 2 £50 (£35) 🛏 2 £35
✳ ▣ V 🔥 🌑 O 🚲 DRY ▣ 🚗
👣 ★★★★ Some rooms en-suite

White Mark Farm *closed 31 Oct - 1 Mar* Δ

Mrs D Bacon
82 Hill Road, Watlington OX49 5AF
T: 01491 612295
Δ 50 £5/person 🚐 5 £5/person 🏠
🚰 🛈 📋 🚲

Section 5

Watlington to Wendover

This 17 miles (27.2km) stretch is probably the most strenuous part of The Ridgeway. It starts out gently enough following the wide track of the Icknield Way but once it departs from this it climbs in and out of several Chilterns valleys. Passing through some lovely nature reserves the Trail reaches a high point with fantastic views at Coombe Hill before descending to Wendover. If you haven't already seen a red kite, you're guaranteed to see one on this stretch!

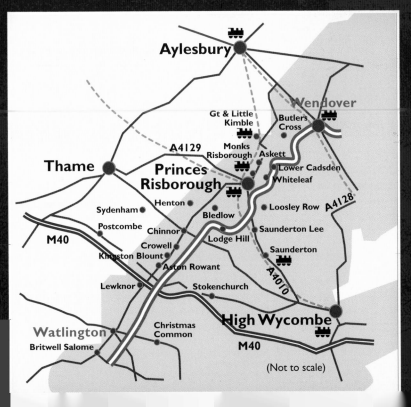

Aylesbury

Wendover

Gt & Little Kimble

Butlers Cross

A4129

Monks Risborough

Askett

Thame

Princes Risborough

Lower Cadsden

Whiteleaf

Henton

Loosley Row

A4128

Sydenham

Bledlow

Postcombe

Chinnor

Saunderton Lee

M40

Crowell

Lodge Hill

Kingston Blount

Saunderton

Aston Rowant

A4010

Lewknor

Stokenchurch

Watlington

Christmas Common

High Wycombe

Britwell Salome

M40

(Not to scale)

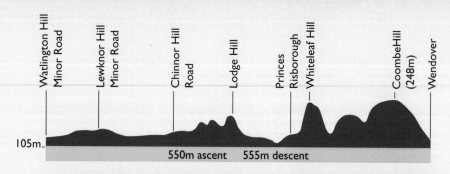

105m—

550m ascent   555m descent

Maps

Landranger maps	175	Reading and Windsor
	165	Aylesbury and Leighton Buzzard
Explorer maps	171	Chiltern Hills West
	181	Chiltern Hills North

Taxis

Place	Name	Telephone Number
Ewelme	Busher's Taxis	01491 826161
Chinnor	Chinnor Cabs	01844 353637
	D & J Cabs	01844 353344
	RCR Private Hire	01844 354334
Loosley Row	Springline Cars	01844 274474
Princes Risborough	Risborough Cars	01844 274111
	Village Cars	01844 342551
	B&V Taxis	01844 342079
	Red Line Cars	01844 343736
Wendover	Alexander's at Wendover	01296 620888

Car Parking

If you choose to park in villages close to The Ridgeway, please park considerately. Other places to park are listed below but you need to be aware that theft from cars parked in the countryside does occur. You are advised to leave any unnecessary items at home or, failing that, ensure that anything valuable is locked in the boot of your vehicle.

Place	Map Grid Reference
On Ridgeway on east side of minor road to Bledlow Ridge 1/2 mile (1km) south of Chinnor	SP 761003
Princes Risborough public car park	SP 810034
Whiteleaf car park, 1/2 mile (1km) east of Princes Risborough. Turn right off A4010 at Monks Risborough and car park is on left at top of escarpment	SP 824036

Place	Map Grid Reference
National Trust car park for Coombe Hill, 1 mile (2km) southwest of Wendover. From Wendover travel west on minor road to Princes Risborough. Take first left, then first left again. At top of hill car park is on left	SP 852062
Wendover public car park	SP 868077

Water Points

Place	Map Grid Reference
White Mark Farm Camp Site, Watlington (March - October)	SU 697939

Toilets

Place	Map Grid Reference
Watlington (High Street)	SU 689945
White Mark Farm Camp Site, Watlington (March- October)	SU 697939
Princes Risborough (Horn Mill Car Park)	SP 809033
Wendover (Library Car Park)	SP 868078

Vets

* large animal vet

Place	Name	Telephone Number
Watlington	Crossroads Veterinary Centre	01491 612799
Stokenchurch	Hall Place Veterinary Centre*	01494 485855
Princes Risborough	Sprinz & Nash	01844 345655
Halton	Wendover Heights Veterinary Centre	01296 623439

Farriers

Place	Name	Telephone Number
Watlington	William Smith	01491 612872
	Adrian Spilsbury	07968 065991
Chinnor	DM Goth	07734 113045
	N Kilner	07867 521476
	Malcolm Woodward	07831 616654
Stokenchurch	John Jennings	07836 562784
	David Matthews	01494 484413
	Jonathan Smith	07717 292445

Saddlers

Place	Name	Telephone Number
Watlington	Cowboy Magic	01491 614960
Chinnor	Gommes	01844 355800
Stokenchurch	Dobbins Clobber	01494 484106

Bike Repairs

Place	Name	Telephone Number
Thame	Thame Cycles	01844 261520
Princes Risborough	Boltons Bikes and Tandems	01844 345949

Mountain Bike Hire

Place	Name	Telephone Number
Princes Risborough	Boltons Bikes and Tandems	01844 345949

Tourist Information Centres

These TICs are staffed but note that many libraries in the area have leaflets about local attractions and events.

★ offers accommodation booking service (until 15:30)

Place	Address/Opening Hours
Wallingford	Wallingford TIC, Town Hall, Market Place, Wallingford OX10 0EG **T**: 01491 826972 **F**: 01491 832925 **W**: www.sodc.com Opening hours: Call in advance to check
Princes Risborough	Princes Risborough Information Centre, Tower Court, Horns Lane, Princes Risborough HP27 0AJ **T**: 01844 274795 **F**: 01844 275795 **E**: risborough_office@wycombe.gov.uk **W**: www.princesrisborough.com Opening hours: All year: Mon-Fri 09:00-17:00
★ Wendover	The Clock Tower, High Street, Wendover HP22 6DU **T**: 01296 696759 **F**: 0871 2361551 **E**: tourism@wendover-pc.gov.uk **W**: www.chilternweb.co.uk/wendover Opening hours: All year: Mon-Sat 10:00-16:00

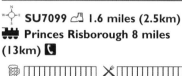

CHRISTMAS COMMON

 **SU7193** ⌂ 1.3 miles (2.1km)
🚂 **Henley-on-Thames 9.6 miles (15.4km)** 📞

🍺 ▯▯▯▯▯▯▯▯▯▯▯ ✕▯▯▯▯▯▯▯▯▯▯▯
S M T W T F S   S M T W T F S

Pub: Fox & Hounds 01491 612599

LEWKNOR

 **SU7197** ⌂ 0.6 miles (1km)
🚂 **Princes Risborough 7 miles (12km)** 📞

🍺 ▯▯▯▯▯▯▯▯▯▯▯ ✕▯▯▯▯▯▯▯▯▯▯▯
S M T W T F S   S M T W T F S

Pub: Leathern Bottle 01844 351482

☆ Chiltern Sculpture Trail
T: 01865 778918 www.
chilternsculpturetrail.co.uk

B&B | Moorcourt Cottage

Mrs Eppy Hodgson
Weston Road, Lewknor OX49 5RU
T: 01844 351419
E: moorcourt2002@yahoo.co.uk
🛏 1 £60 🛏 1 £60 (£37) ♛♙ V
⚲ 🚲 **DRY** ⊡ 🚗 ♿ ★★★★ All
rooms en-suite

POSTCOMBE

 **SU7099** ⌂ 1.6 miles (2.5km)
🚂 **Princes Risborough 8 miles (13km)** 📞

🍺 ▯▯▯▯▯▯▯▯▯▯▯ ✕▯▯▯▯▯▯▯▯▯▯▯
S M T W T F S   S M T W T F S

🧺 ▯▯▯▯▯▯▯▯▯▯▯
S M T W T F S

Pub: England's Rose 01844 281383

Beech Farm | B&B

Mrs Jackie Graham
Salt Lane, Postcombe, Thame OX9 7EE
T: 01844 281240 **M:** 07973 506443
E: beech.farm@btopenworld.com
www.beechfarm.co.uk
🛏 2 £60 (£40) 🛏 1 £40 ♛♙ 🏠 V ⚲
🍴 🚲 **DRY** ⊡ 🚗 ♿ ★★★★ All
rooms en-suite

View over the Chilterns

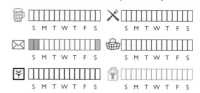

ASTON ROWANT

SU7298 △ **0.6 miles (1km)**
Princes Risborough 6 miles (10km) ☎

🍺 |||||||||||| ✕ |||||||||||||
   S M T W T F S   S M T W T F S

Pub: Lambert Arms 01844 351496
(closed Feb - June 2008 for renovation)

☆ Aston Rowant National Nature
Reserve
T: 01844 351833
www.naturalengland.org.uk

B&B **Tower Cottage** *closed Xmas & New Year*

Mrs Margaret Mason
Chinnor Road, Aston Rowant
OX49 5SH
T: 01844 354676
E: towercottagebb@aol.com
www.tower-cottage.co.uk
🛏 2 £50 🛏 1 £50 🛏 1 £70 (£40)
⚥ 🖥 V 🏕 🚲 DRY 🅾 🚶 Some
rooms en-suite

INN **Lambert Arms**

Miss Sarah Deakin
London Road, Aston Rowant OX49 5SB
T: 01844 353496 **F:** 01844 351893
E: info@lambertarms.co.uk
www.lambertarms.co.uk
🛏 7 £65 🛏 1 £105 (£65) 🛏 1 £50
⚥ ♿ 🖥 V 🏕 🍷 🍴 🚗 VISA Most
major cards. Some rooms en-suite

STOKENCHURCH

SU7696 △ **2.7 miles (4.3km)**
Princes Risborough or High Wycombe 7.3 miles (11.7km) ☎

🍺 |||||||||||| ✕ |||||||||||||
   S M T W T F S   S M T W T F S

✉ |||||||||||| 🧺 |||||||||||||
   S M T W T F S   S M T W T F S

🗓 |||||||||||| 🏧 |||||||||||||
   S M T W T F S   S M T W T F S

£ Lloyds TSB & two 🆒 in local stores

Hallbottom Farm   B&B

Mrs Deborah Abbot
Park Lane, Stokenchurch HP14 3TQ
T: 01494 482520 **M:** 07778 216024
E: deborah@hallbottomfarm.co.uk
www.hallbottomfarm.co.uk
🛏 4 £75 🛏 2 £75 🛏 1 £110
(£45) ⚥ (over 6) ♿ V 🍴 🅾 🚲 DRY
★★★★ Some rooms en-suite

KINGSTON BLOUNT

✥ **SU7399** 👢 **0.5 miles (0.8km)**
🚂 **Princes Risborough 6 miles (10km)** 📞

🍺 ☰☰☰☰☰☰☰☰☰ ✗☰☰☰☰☰☰☰☰☰
　 S M T W T F S 　 S M T W T F S

Pub: Cherry Tree 01844 352273

B&B | **Lakeside Town Farm**

Mrs Clark
Town Farm Cottage, Brook Street,
Kingston Blount OX39 4RZ
T/F: 01844 352152 **M:** 07971 436504
E: townfarmcottage@oxfree.com
www.townfarmcottage.co.uk
🛏 1 £70 🛏 1 £80 🛏 1 £80 (£55)
👫 (over 9) **V** 🚲 **DRY** 💳 Most
major cards ★★★★ All rooms en-suite

Cherry Tree  🏨

Mr Dalla-Costa
High Street, Kingston Blount OX39 4SJ
T: 01844 352273
E: cherrytreepub@btinternet.com
www.thecherrytreepub.com
🛏 3 £70 🛏 1 £70 (£60) 🛏 4 £60
♿ **V** 🍷 🕯 **VISA** Most major cards
★★★ All rooms en-suite

CROWELL

✥ **SU7499** 👢 **0.5 miles (0.8km)**
🚂 **Princes Risborough 5.6 miles (9km)**

🍺 ☰☰☰☰☰☰☰☰☰ ✗☰☰☰☰☰☰☰☰☰
　 S M T W T F S 　 S M T W T F S

Pub: Shepherd's Crook 01844 351431

Walkers near Kingston Blount

CHINNOR

 SP7500 🏕 0.6 miles (1km)
🚂 Princes Risborough 4 miles
(7km) P F 📞 👬 ♿WC

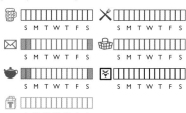

🅿 in Co-op

☆ Chinnor Hill Nature Reserve
T: 01865 775476 www.bbowt.org.uk

☆ Chinnor and Princes Risborough
Railway
T: 01844 353535 www.cprra.co.uk

SC **Cherry Orchard**

Mrs Jill Robertson
Hill Top Lane, Hill Top, Chinnor OX39
4BH
T: 01844 354208 **M:** 07801 257187
F: 01844 352218
E: creativecopper@btopenworld.com
Self-catering studio flat, sleeps 2, £30/
person (includes supplies for non-
cooked breakfast) 🚲

Croft *closed 20 Dec-May* B&B

Mrs Beth Smith
Chinnor Hill, Chinnor OX39 4BS
T: 01844 353654 **M:** 07941 697873
E: beth@acornhomesltd.co.uk
www.bethatthecroft.co.uk
🛏 2 £50 (£38) 👫 🚩 V ♦ O 🚲
DRY ⊙ 🚗 🐾 ★★★★ One room
en-suite
🅷 Payment by cash or cheque only

Station Road Bed & Breakfast B&B

Mr Peter Snow
7 Station Road, Chinnor OX39 4PU
T/F: 01844 351889
E: peter@snow2258.fsnet.co.uk
🛏 2 £45 (£30) 🛏 1 £30 👫 🚩 V ♫
♦ 🚲 DRY ⊙ 🐾

HENTON

 SP7602 🏕 1 miles (1.5km)
🚂 Princes Risborough 3 miles
(5km) 📞

Pub: Peacock 01844 353519

Manor Farm Cottage B&B

Mr & Mrs Trevor & Jean Dixon
Henton, Chinnor OX39 4AE
T: 01844 353301 **M:** 07889 441601
E: dixonhenton@aol.com
www.manorfarmcottage.info
🛏 1 £55 🛏 1 £55 (£38) 👫 🚩 V
♫ ♦ O 🚲 DRY ⊙ 🐾 ★★★★

Peacock

Mrs Naetha Uren
Henton, Chinnor OX39 4AH
T: 01844 353519 **F:** 01844 353891
E: info@peacock.uk.com
www.peacock.uk.com

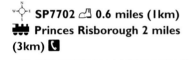 24 £85 (£75) | £75

V Most major cards. All rooms en-suite

BLEDLOW

SP7702 0.6 miles (1km)
Princes Risborough 2 miles (3km)

🍺 ||||||||||| ✕|||||||||||
  S M T W T F S   S M T W T F S

Pub: Lions of Bledlow 01844 343345

☆ Lyde Gardens (next to church) open daily dawn to dusk.

LODGE HILL

SP7900 on path
Princes Risborough 2 miles (3km)

Old Callow Down Farm B&B

GR SU787000 100m from Ridgeway
Mr & Mrs C J Gee
Wigans Lane, Bledlow Ridge, High Wycombe HP14 4BH
T: 01844 344416 **F:** 01844 344703
E: oldcallow@aol.com
www.chilternscottage.co.uk

1 £55 (£35)

DRY Room is en-suite

SAUNDERTON LEE

SP7901 0.6 miles (1km)
Saunderton 1.2 miles (2km)

🍺 |||||||||||| ✕||||||||||||
  S M T W T F S   S M T W T F S

Pub: Rose & Crown 01844 345299

View from Chinnor Hill

LOOSLEY ROW

SP8100 1.1 miles (1.7km)
Saunderton 2.4 miles (3.8km)

B&B SC | Greenhills Garden Apartment

Mrs D O Dean
Greenhills, Little Lane, Loosley Row,
Princes Risborough HP27 0NX
T: 01844 342409 **M:** 07940 211079
E: dormic@aol.com
1 £70 2 £90 (£55)
All major cards. All rooms en-suite
Self-catering accommodation available from £70/night for 2 sharing

PRINCES RISBOROUGH

SP8003 on path
Princes Risborough

Town with full range of services, visit www.visitbuckinghamshire.org for further details. Farmers Market 3rd Thurs of each month.

☆ Princes Risborough Manor House
T: 01494 755573 www.nationaltrust.org.uk

Drifters Lodge *closed Xmas & New Year* | B&B

Ms Christine Williams
60 Picts, Princes Risborough HP27 9DX
T: 01844 274773 **M:** 07801 482656
E: info@driftceslodge.co.uk
www.driftceslodge.co.uk
1 £60 2 £60 (£40) (over 9)
Mastercard, Visa, Maestro ★★★★
All rooms en-suite

Coppins B&B | B&B

Mrs Jill Thomas
New Road, Princes Risborough HP27 0LA
T: 01844 344508 **M:** 07745 596103
E: jillthomas@thecoppins.co.uk
www.thecoppins.co.uk
2 £55 (£35) (over 4)
★★
Twin rooms can be made into double rooms. VisitBritain Silver Award

---

Black Prince | INN

Mr Simon Keen
86 Wycombe Road, Princes Risborough HP27 0EN
T: 01844 345569
4 £64 2 £64 (£47) 3 £47
Most major cards. All rooms en-suite

B SC **Ridgeway Lodge**

Mrs Miv Hughes
Upper Icknield Way, Saunderton, Princes
Risborough HP27 9NL
T: 01844 3454387 **M:** 07738 587480
E: moh@jghughes1.f9.co.uk
www.bedbreakfast-ridgewaylodge.co.uk
🛏 1 £60 🛏 2 £65 (£35) 👫(over 5)
♿ 📷 V 🏊 🚲 DRY ⭕ Some rooms
en-suite.
🍴 Self-catering also available, £80

WHITELEAF

⊕ SP8204 👢 0.6 miles (1km)
🚆 Monks Risborough 1 miles
(1.5km)

Pub: Red Lion 01844 344476

☆ Whiteleaf Hill and Cross
www.buckscc.gov.uk/countryside/whiteleaf

LOWER CADSDEN

⊕ SP8204 👢 on path
🚆 Monks Risborough 1 miles
(2km)

Pub: Plough at Cadsden 01844 343302

☆ Grangelands and Pulpit Hill Nature
Reserve www.nationaltrust.org.uk

ASKETT

⊕ SP8105 👢 1.2 miles (2km)
🚆 Monks Risborough 0.5 miles
(1km) 📞

Solis Ortu   B&B

Mrs Pamela Crockett
Aylesbury Road, Askett, Princes
Risborough HP27 9LY
T: 01844 347777 **F:** 01844 343509
E: pamela@crockettandson.co.uk
🛏 1 £50 🛏 1 £50 (£25) 👫 (over
9) V 🏊 🚲 🚐 ★★★
🍴 Private bathroom available

GREAT KIMBLE

⊕ SU8206 👢 0.6 miles (1km)
🚆 Little Kimble 0.5 miles (1km)
📞

Pubs: Swan 01844 275288 & Bernard
Arms 01844 346172

Swan at Great Kimble   INN

Mr Tim Woolnough
Grove Lane, Great Kimble, Aylesbury
HP17 9TR
T: 01844 275288 **E:** theswangtkimble@
aol.com
🛏 1 £70 🛏 2 £60 🛏 1 £100
(£40) 👫 V 🏊 🌙 ⓘ DRY VISA Most
major cards. All rooms en-suite

BUTLERS CROSS

SP8407 ⌂ **0.6 miles (1km)**
🚂 **Little Kimble 1 miles (2km)** 📞

🗇 ⫴⫴⫴⫴⫴⫴⫴ ✕ ⫴⫴⫴⫴⫴⫴⫴
S M T W T F S   S M T W T F S

Pub: Russell Arms 01296 622618

☆ Chiltern Brewery
T: 01296 613647
www.chilternbrewery.co.uk

WENDOVER

SP8607 ⌂ **on path**
🚂 **Wendover** ℹ

Town with full range of services, visit
www.visitbuckinghamshire.org for
further details. Farmers Market 3rd Sat
of each month.

☆ Wendover Woods
T: 01420 520212
www.forestry.gov.uk

Dunsmore Edge *closed Xmas & New Year* B&B

Mr & Mrs Ron & Ursula Drackford
Dunsmore Lane, London Road,
Wendover HP22 6PN
T: 01296 623080 **E:** uron@lineone.net
🛏 1 £52 🛏 1 £55 (£30) 🛏 1 £30
👫 (over 4) ♿ V 🅿 🚲 **DRY** ★★★
Some rooms en-suite

Mrs MacDonald's *closed Xmas & New Year* B&B

Mrs Yvonne MacDonald
25 Witchell, Wendover HP22 6EG
T: 01296 623426
🛏 1 £62 (£37) 🛏 1 £32 🌮 V 🅿
🚲 **DRY** 🔲 🐕 ★★★
🚽 Private bathroom available

Ramblers Retreat *closed weekdays in school term* ▲

Ms Julianne Wilderspin
Wendover House School, Church Lane,
Wendover HP22 6NL
T: 01296 622157 **F:** 01296 622628
E: jwilderspin@bucksgfl.org.uk
www.wendoverhouse.bucks.sch.uk
🛏 6 £15 including bedding pack (£12
without) 👫
🚽 Kitchen available for self-catering
breakfast. Booking in advance essential

**Monument on Coombe Hill
above Wendover**

Section 6

Wendover to
Ivinghoe Beacon

This 11.8 miles (18.8km) section is the most wooded of
The Ridgeway with extensive woods, many of beech, much of the
way. However once the Trail reaches Pitstone Hill the final few miles
are in open downland countryside reminiscent of the landscape
surrounding earlier stages. As a final flourish The Ridgeway finishes
on top of yet another Iron Age fort at Ivinghoe Beacon.

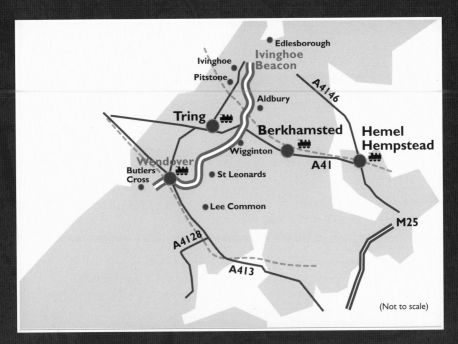

(Not to scale)

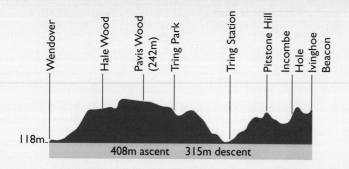

118m

408m ascent   315m descent

Maps

| Landranger maps | 165 | Aylesbury and Leighton Buzzard |
| Explorer maps | 181 | Chiltern Hills North |

Taxis

Place	Name	Telephone Number
Wendover	Alexander's at Wendover	01296 620888
Wigginton	T C Cabs	01442 875757
Wigginton	Diamond Cars	01442 890303
Tring	AAA Line Taxis	01442 890288
	Airport Taxis of Tring	01442 828848
	Aky Cars of Tring	01442 891234
	Bev's Cars	01442 890003
	DMG	01442 824105
	John Taxi's	01442 828828
	Mike's Private Hire	01442 826161

Car Parking

If you choose to park in villages close to The Ridgeway, please park considerately.
Other places to park are listed below but you need to be aware that theft
from cars parked in the countryside does occur. You are advised to leave any
unnecessary items at home or, failing that, ensure that anything valuable is locked in
the boot of your vehicle.

Place	Map Grid Reference
Wendover public car park	SP 868077
Pitstone Hill car park east of Tring. From sharp bend on B488, 1/2 mile (1km) southeast of Ivinghoe, take minor road signposted Aldbury. Car park is on right after 1/2 mile (1km)	SP 955149
National Trust car park for Ivinghoe Beacon, on the left of minor road to Ringshall, 1/2 mile (1km) south off the B489	SP 962162

Toilets

Place	Map Grid Reference
Wendover (Library Car Park)	SP 868078

Vets

Place	Name	Telephone Number
Halton	Wendover Heights Veterinary Centre	01296 623439
Tring	Springwell Veterinary Surgery	01442 822151

Tourist Information Centres

These TICs are staffed but note that many libraries in the area have leaflets about local attractions and events.

★ offers accommodation booking service (until 15:30)

Place	Address/Opening Hours
★Wendover	The Clock Tower, High Street, Wendover HP22 6DU **T**: 01296 696759 **F**: 0871 2361551 **E**: tourism@wendover-pc.gov.uk **W**: www.chilternweb.co.uk/wendover Opening hours: All year: Mon-Sat 10:00-16:00
Tring	99 Akeman Street, Tring HP23 6AA **T**: 01442 823347 **F**: 01442 827178 **E**: info@tring.gov.uk **W**: www.tring.gov.uk Opening hours: All year: Mon-Sat 09:30-15:00, Sat 10:00-13:00

Ivinghoe Beacon from Pitstone Hill

LEE COMMON

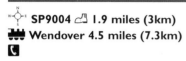 **SP9004** 1.9 miles (3km)
Wendover 4.5 miles (7.3km)
📞

S M T W T F S   S M T W T F S

B&B SC | Lower Bassibones Farm

Mrs Anthea Hartley
Lee Common, Great Missenden
HP16 9LA
T: 01494 837798 **F:** 01494 837778
E: lowerbassibones@yahoo.co.uk
http://discover-real-england.com
🛏 2 £65 🚶 (over 11) **V** 🚲 **DRY**
💻 **VISA** Most major cards ★★★★ One
room en-suite
Self-catering accommodation also
available at £295/week ★★★★

ST LEONARDS

SP9107 0.9 miles (1.5km)
Wendover 3 miles (5km) 📞

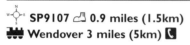
S M T W T F S   S M T W T F S

Pub: White Lion 01494 758387

Field Cottage   *closed Xmas & New Year* B&B

Mrs Sue Jepson
St Leonards, Tring HP23 6NS
T: 01494 837602
E: michael.jepson@lineone.net
www.fieldcottagebandb.co.uk
🛏 1 £65 🚶 1 £65 (£50) 💤 1 £40
🚶 (over 11) **V** 🍎 **O** 🚲 **DRY** Some
rooms en-suite

WIGGINTON

SP9310 on path
Tring 1 miles (2km) 📞

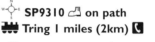
S M T W T F S   S M T W T F S

S M T W T F S

Pub: Greyhound Inn 01442 824631

☆ Tring Park
www.tring.gov.uk/info/tpark.htm

Greyhound Inn   INN

Mr Paul Phillips
Chesham Road, Wigginton HP23 6EH
T: 01442 824631
E: the-greyhound@hotmail.com
www.the-greyhound.co.uk
🛏 3 £60 🚶 1 £75 (£45) 🚶 ♿ **V**
🚲 🍺 🍎 **VISA** Most major cards. All
rooms en-suite

The Greyhound

Wigginton
Tel 01442 824631

You can be sure of a warm welcome at The Greyhound, Wigginton which is ideally situated for The Ridgeway.

All rooms are single/double/family with private en-suite shower rooms, television, wireless internet access and tea and coffee making facilities.

We pride ourselves on serving delicious home cooked food from a varied menu which includes char grilled aberdeen angus steaks and burgers or lighter bites. We also have a choice of real ales, chilled beers and wines.

Packed lunches are also available if required.

B&B | **Rangers Cottage**

Mrs Sally Dawson
Tring Park, Wigginton, Tring HP23 6EB
T: 01442 890155 **F:** 01442 827814
E: rangerscottage@aol.com
www.rangerscottage.com
🛏 2 £75 👢 1 £75 (£65) ⛌ V 🚲
DRY 💳 Mastercard, Visa ★★★★ All
rooms en-suite
🍴 Cooked breakfast weekends only
(£5 supplement/person), continental
breakfast weedays.

TRING

⊕ **SP9211** 🥾 1.2 miles (2km)
🚃 Tring P£ 🚻

Town with full range of services, visit
www.tring.gov.uk for further details.

☆ The Walter Rothschild Zoological
Museum
T: 0207 9426171
www.nhm.ac.uk/visit-us/galleries/tring

☆ Grand Union Canal
www.waterscape.com/
Grand_Union_Canal

☆ Duchies Piece Nature Reserve
www.wildlifetrust.org.uk/herts/reserves

Pendley Manor Hotel 🏨

Mrs Claire Lee
Cow Lane, Tring HP23 5QY
T: 01442 891891 **F:** 01442 890687
E: sales@pendley-manor.co.uk
www.pendley-manor.co.uk
🛏 55 £110 👢 15 £110 👢 2 £110
👢 1 £85 ⊖ ⛌ ♿V 🐾 🐕 O 🍴 💳
Most major cards ★★★★ All rooms
en-suite

Rose and Crown Hotel 🏨

Mrs Claire Lee
High Street, Tring HP23 5AH
T: 01442 824071 **F:** 01442 890735
E: salesrose.crown@pendley-manor.
co.uk
🛏 18 £90 👢 2 £90 👢 3 £90 👢
4 £85 ⊖ ⛌ 📷 V 🐾 🐕 i 🍴 💳 Most
major cards ★★★ All rooms en-suite

Greyhound Inn, Aldbury

ALDBURY

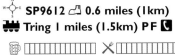 **SP9612** 0.6 miles (1km)
🚂 Tring 1 miles (1.5km) P F 📞

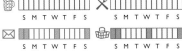

Pubs: Greyhound 01442 851228 &
Valiant Trooper 01442 851203

☆ Ashridge Estate
T: 01494 755557
www.nationaltrust.org.uk

B&B | **16 Stoneycroft** | *closed Xmas*

Mrs Sandra Crannage
Aldbury, Tring HP23 5RL
T/F: 01442 851294 **M:** 07801 846351
🛏 1 £50 🛏 1 £50 (£25) 🛏 1 £25
🚻 📷 V 🎿 🚲 **DRY** 🚗 🛶

INN | **Greyhound Inn**

Mr Tim O'Gorman
Aldbury, Tring HP23 5RT
T: 01442 851228 **F:** 01442 851495
www.greyhoundaldbury.co.uk
🛏 8 £75 (£65) 🚻 🛄 📷 V 🎿 🚲
🚲 🛶 **VISA** Mastercard, Visa, Delta. All
rooms en-suite

PITSTONE

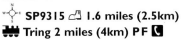 **SP9315** 1.6 miles (2.5km)
🚂 Tring 2 miles (4km) P F 📞

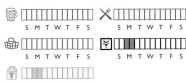

💷 In general store
Pubs: Bell 01296 668078 & Duke of
Wellington 01296 661402

☆ Pitstone Windmill
www.nationaltrust.org.uk

☆ Pitstone Green Museum
T: 01494 528051 http://website.lineone.
net/~pitstonemus

Near Aldbury Nowers

IVINGHOE

SP9416 🛏 **0.9 miles (1.5km)**
🚌 **Tring 3 miles (5km)** 📞

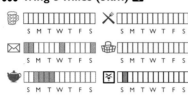

🖼 In post office
Pub: Rose & Crown 01296 668472
☆ Ford End Water Mill
T: 01296 660436
www.fordendwatermill.co.uk

SC | **Town Farm**

GR SP950164 0.9 miles (1.4km)
from Ridgeway
Mrs Leach
Ivinghoe, Leighton Buzzard LU7 9EL
T: 01296 608455 **M:** 07984 418914
F: 01296 662836
E: info@letsunlimited.com
www.letsunlimited.com
1 bedroom and 3 bedroom cottages
available for holiday let

Mastercard, Visa, American Express,
Delta ★★★

Silver Birch Campsite | *closed 1 Dec - 31 March* ⛺

Mrs Jane Rance
Upper Icknield Way, Ivinghoe, Leighton
Buzzard LU7 9EN
T: 01296 668348 **M:** 07760 491880
⛺ 10 £3/person ▫ ♿WC 🚲

EDLESBOROUGH

SP9719 🛏 **1.9 miles (3km)**
🚌 **Tring 6 miles (9km) P F** 📞

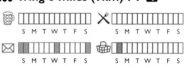

Pub: Bell 01525 222957

Ridgeway End | *closed Xmas* B&B

Mrs Judith Lloyd
5 Ivinghoe Way, Edlesborough,
Dunstable LU6 2EL
T/F: 01525 220405 **M:** 07721 027339
E: judy.lloyd@tesco.net
🛏 1 £50 🛏 1 £50 🛏 1 £50 (£35)

All rooms en-suite

94

Aldbourne	46	Liddington	46
Aldbury	93	Lockeridge	35
Aldworth	62	Lockinge	57
Ardington	58	Lodge Hill	83
Ashbury	47	Loosley Row	84
Askett	85	Lower Cadsden	85
Aston Rowant	80	Marlborough	35
Avebury	36	Moulsford	62
Barbury Castle	37	Nettlebed	72
Bishopstone	46	North Stoke	70
Bledlow	83	Nuffield	72
Blewbury	60	Ogbourne St George	38
Britwell Salome	74	Park Corner	73
Broad Hinton	37	Pitstone	93
Butlers Cross	86	Postcombe	79
Chilton	59	Princes Risborough	84
Chinnor	82	St Leonards	90
Chiseldon	38	Saunderton Lee	83
Christmas Common	79	South Stoke	70
Compton	60	Sparsholt	50
Cookley Green	73	Stokenchurch	80
Crowell	81	Streatley	62
Crowmarsh Gifford	70	Tring	92
East Hendred	58	Uffington	48
East Ilsley	59	Upton	60
East Kennett	35	Wallingford	71
Edlesborough	94	Wanborough	46
Ewelme	73	Wantage	57
Farnborough	58	Watlington	74
Goring-on-Thames	69	Wendover	86
Great Kimble	85	West Hendred	58
Hailey	72	West Ilsley	59
Henton	82	West Overton	35
Ivinghoe	94	Whiteleaf	85
Kingston Blount	81	Wigginton	90
Kingston Lisle	49	Winterbourne Bassett	36
Lee Common	90	Winterbourne Monkton	36
Letcombe Regis	56	Woolstone	48
Lewknor	79	Wroughton	37

Distances between places along the The Ridgeway in miles

	Overton Hill	Ogbourne St George	Fox Hill	Uffington Castle	Sparsholt Firs	A338 (Wantage)	Bury Down	Streatley	Mongewell Park	Nuffield	Watlington	Chinnor	Princes Risborough	Wendover	Wigginton
Ogbourne St George	9.3														
Fox Hill	17.0	7.7													
Uffington Castle	22.3	13.0	5.3												
Sparsholt Firs	25.3	16.0	8.3	3.0											
A338 (Wantage)	29.1	19.8	12.1	6.8	3.8										
Bury Down	34.5	25.2	17.5	12.2	9.2	5.4									
Streatley	42.7	33.4	25.7	20.4	17.4	13.6	8.2								
Mongewell Park	48.5	39.2	31.5	26.2	23.2	19.4	14.0	5.8							
Nuffield	52.4	43.1	35.4	30.1	27.1	23.3	17.9	9.7	3.9						
Watlington	58.0	48.7	41.0	35.7	32.7	28.9	23.5	15.3	9.5	5.6					
Chinnor	63.7	54.4	46.7	41.4	38.4	34.6	29.2	21.0	15.2	11.3	5.7				
Princes Risborough	68.5	59.2	51.5	46.2	43.2	39.4	34.0	25.8	20.0	16.1	10.5	4.8			
Wendover	75.0	65.7	58.0	52.7	49.7	45.9	40.5	32.3	26.5	22.6	17.0	11.3	6.5		
Wigginton	81.5	72.2	64.5	59.2	56.2	52.4	47.0	38.8	33.0	29.1	23.5	17.8	13.0	6.5	
Ivinghoe Beacon	86.8	77.5	69.8	64.5	61.5	57.7	52.3	44.1	38.3	34.4	28.8	23.1	18.3	11.8	5.3